Robert C. Jenkins, Carlo Tommaso Maillard de Tournon

**The Jesuits in China and the Legation of Cardinal de Tournon**

An Examination of conflicting Evidence and an Attempt at an impartial Judgment

Robert C. Jenkins, Carlo Tommaso Maillard de Tournon

**The Jesuits in China and the Legation of Cardinal de Tournon**
*An Examination of conflicting Evidence and an Attempt at an impartial Judgment*

ISBN/EAN: 9783743358133

Manufactured in Europe, USA, Canada, Australia, Japa

Cover: Foto ©Lupo / pixelio.de

Manufactured and distributed by brebook publishing software (www.brebook.com)

Robert C. Jenkins, Carlo Tommaso Maillard de Tournon

**The Jesuits in China and the Legation of Cardinal de Tournon**

# THE JESUITS IN CHINA

AND

## THE LEGATION OF CARDINAL DE TOURNON

*AN EXAMINATION OF CONFLICTING EVIDENCE AND AN ATTEMPT AT AN IMPARTIAL JUDGMENT*

BY

ROBERT C. JENKINS, M.A.

RECTOR AND VICAR OF LYMINGE, HON. CANON OF CANTERBURY

"*Finita est causa sed nondum finitur error. Destructur missio antequam reformetur*"
EP. CARD. DE TOURNON AD P. GERDILLONEM

LONDON
DAVID NUTT, 270–271, STRAND
1894

*TO*

*THE RIGHT HONOURABLE*

*THE VICE-CHANCELLOR SIR JAMES BACON*

*IN GRATEFUL AND AFFECTIONATE*

*REMEMBRANCE OF A*

*FRIENDSHIP OF MORE THAN*

*FIFTY YEARS.*

# CONTENTS

| CHAP. | | PAGE |
|---|---|---|
| | INTRODUCTION | 1 |
| I. | FATHER MATTEO RICCI—ORIGIN OF THE CONTROVERSY, A.D. 1582-1612 | 9 |
| II. | THE REFERENCE TO THE CONGREGATIONS | 18 |
| III. | THE APPEAL TO ROME | 31 |
| IV. | THE CHOICE OF A LEGATE—CHARLES MAILLARD DE TOURNON | 38 |
| V. | THE RELATION OF SIGNOR ANGELITA OF THE ALLEGED ATTEMPT TO POISON THE LEGATE | 46 |
| VI. | THE RELATION OF THE ABATE SALA | 55 |
| VII. | SIGNOR APPIANI THE INTERPRETER OF THE LEGATE | 74 |
| VIII. | THE JESUIT DEFENCE | 83 |
| IX. | THE IMPERIAL DECREE | 103 |
| X. | THE LEGATE A PRISONER AT MACAO | 115 |
| XI. | THE QUESTION IN REGARD TO THE COURT OF ROME | 151 |

## *ILLUSTRATIONS.*

| | |
|---|---|
| PORTRAIT OF CARDINAL TOURNON | *Frontispiece* |
| PORTRAIT OF CAM-HY | *To face page* 9 |

# THE JESUITS IN CHINA

## INTRODUCTION

THE controversy on the Chinese Rites which agitated the Church of Rome during the seventeenth and eighteenth centuries, is one which, as it involved the interests as well as the orthodoxy of the religious orders and even the veracity of the disputants, can never be impartially treated by a member of the Roman Communion. The bitterness with which it was carried on for more than a century, the voluminous extent of the documentary evidence and of the argumentative treatises which have been written upon it, which form a library in themselves, and the almost hand-to-hand conflict of the witnesses, render the impartial judgment of the whole case, to those interested impossible, and to the most disinterested, a work of extreme difficulty. The too prevailing readiness in every case in which the Jesuits are concerned to condemn them unheard, and to believe that wherever there is a conflict of evidence the truth must be on the side of their opponents—a readiness as visible in the rival orders of the Roman Church as it is in the Protestant world—has ever been a fatal obstacle to the fair and equitable judgment of a case so singularly complicated; while the settlement of the controversy by the Papal confirmation of all the acts and decisions of the Legate, has closed the lips of the "Society," now more than ever zealous to uphold the autocracy of the infallible See.

But the controversy though thus authoritatively closed is one which is capable of being continually reopened by the exigencies of the missionary work, not only in China, but in other lands. Even among Protestant missionaries the same difficulties have arisen in our own time in regard to the proper title of the Deity, and the form which it ought to assume in a language absolutely destitute of any definite or distinctive name to express the Supreme Being. Nor is the controversy on the methods of teaching Christianity, and the gradual manner in which its higher doctrines should be introduced to the heathen and the prudence with which its foundations should be laid, less likely to assume the same importance and to involve the same difficulties which were disclosed in the days of the great Father Ricci, and developed in those of his successors. These words of brief introduction cannot be closed without as brief a description of the authorities which have been employed in the endeavour to arrive at a reasonable judgment and estimate of the comparative weight to be attached to the witnesses on either side. The principal authority, and one which is now so rare as to make it desirable to give as full an account of it as our limited space admits, is the collection of original documents, the greater part of them never before published, which came out in eight small 8vo volumes at Venice in 1761--62, printed by Giuseppe Bettinelli. This is, I believe, a prohibited work, probably on account of the charge against the Jesuits of the attempt to poison the Legate.

Its contents may be thus described :—

Vol. I. contains :

1. The original letters of the Legate, twelve in number (of primary importance).
2. Five relations—the first by the Legate himself, the second by his secretary Angelita—the rest apparently by the same, but without any author's name attached. These open with the voyage to China, and end with the death of the Legate in 1710. They are all (except the second) of the greatest importance and interest.
3. Letters of members of the Augustinian and

other orders and of several Cardinals. That of Father Appiani is the most valuable.

Vol. II. Letters and decrees of the Legate with the successive protests they called forth. All these, thirty-three in number, are of the highest value, especially the fourth and fifth, which may be regarded as parallel narrations to those of Angelita and Sala, from the pen of the Legate himself. They are addressed to Cardinal Paolucci, his special Patron in Rome.

Vol. III. Contains sixty-two documents, exhibiting the controversy as carried on by the Legate on the one side and the Emperor and the Jesuits on the other.

Vol. IV. Contains the controversy between Father Antonio Thomas, the Jesuit Advocate, and the Legate. This volume is very important as containing the defence of the Society, and also the still more important relation of the Portuguese Governor of Macao, Don Diego Pinho de Teixeyra, with the criticisms of it written (apparently) by Father Fattinelli.

Vol. V. Contains the correspondence with, and decisions of, the Court of Rome from

1669 to 1710. This collection is of supreme importance.

Vol. VI. Contains the letters from Clement XI. to various Kings, Bishops and others. These are naturally of secondary importance, written as they are from Rome, and with a very imperfect knowledge of the history of the Legation; and rest on the statements of the Legate alone. It also contains an account of the persecutions of the Legate written by an anonymous Franciscan, whose violence of language renders it of very doubtful value to an impartial historian. Far more important is the Cardinal's last letter to his brother the Marquis de Tournon (November 19th, 1708), and Fattinelli's letter of March 9th, 1709, which immediately follows.

Vol. VII. Contains a variety of letters, orations, &c., of Clement XI. and others. One of the most important is the Edict of the Emperor against the Legate, p. 136.

The volume concludes with some observations on the documents contained in the third part of Vol. IV. These seem to have been written by Fattinelli.

Vol. VIII. Contains the relation of the Abate Sala on the events between April 1705 and January 12, 1708.

This is very valuable in connection with this later period, and is written with great moderation.

Such are the contents, and such appears to me to be the relative value, of the vast collection of documents entitled : "*Memorie Storiche dell' Eminentiss. Monsignor Cardinale de Tournon, esposte con monumenti rari ed autentici non più dati alla luce.*"

In addition to these, the following important contributions to the history of the Legation have been examined and confronted together :

I. "Acta causæ Rituum" (Rom. 1704).

II. "Osservazioni sopra la Risposta fatta dal Procuratore del Sig. Cardinal di Tournon à cinque Memoriali del Padre Provana," &c. (This is a defence of the Jesuits, without place or date.)

III. "Apologia della Riposte," &c. A reply to the above on behalf of the Legate.

IV. "La Verità e l'Innocenza de' Missionarj della Compagnia di Giesù." Written in reply to the Apologia above mentioned.

V. "Lo stato presente della Chiesa Cinese." A general defence of the Jesuits, translated from the French.

The five last treatises, which are of considerable length, I possess bound up in a single volume at the time of their production, evidently selected from the crowd of contemporary publications of the same kind, as presenting most clearly and fully the two parties in the controversy, and the strange conflict of their evidence. The aspect which the facts here related presented to the Court of Rome is well described in the life of Clement XI., drawn up (it is believed) by the Abate Polidori under the direction of Cardinal Albano, the nephew of the Pope. Of this we have given extracts in the course of our narrative.

We have also availed ourselves of the valuable contribution of the great Leibnitz to the history of the Chinese Mission, entitled "Novissima Sinica," published in 1699 without mention of place, and with the initials G. G. L. (Godefridus Gulielmus Leibnitz).

Such an investigation involves the trial of the witnesses as well as the critical examination of their testimony, and in order to pronounce a fair judgment, we must dismiss from our minds the prepossessions which the extreme views of the adversaries of the Jesuits and the tragic fate of the Cardinal make it difficult to us to surrender. Of the former, the famous Archbishop of Mechlin, de Pradt, gives us an instance, who in his "Jesuitisme ancien et moderne" attributes to them all the persecutions and even the death of the Cardinal, apparently in ignorance of all that they alleged in their defence, making them the jailers and even the murderers of the unfortunate Legate. The fact that their reign in China was succeeded by that of the Portuguese at Macao is entirely overlooked by those who make these extreme statements. Yet they appear to have been endorsed by Innocent XIII., the successor of Clement XI., in his decree of September 13th, 1725.

# CHAPTER I

### FATHER MATTEO RICCI—ORIGIN OF THE CONTROVERSY, A.D. 1582–1612

THE indomitable resolution of the great St. Francis Xavier after he had completed his work in Japan, to introduce Christianity into China, resisted so long by the Portuguese authorities at Goa and elsewhere, and finally frustrated through the impediments thrown by them in his way, forms at once a mournful and an inspiring incident in the early history of missionary labours in the East, and gave a new and stronger energy to those who took up his great work, suspended for a season, only to be resumed by a successor his equal in zeal, but greatly his superior in learning, Father Matteo Ricci, a member of the same Society. Struck down by a fever when he was at the point of realising the great object of his ambition, Xavier died almost within sight of the country towards which all his hopes had been directed, and bequeathed rather the inspiration of his work than the work itself to others, the executors, as it were, of his last will. The

Franciscans and Dominicans in the meantime had not neglected the field which lay so near to that of their Indian labours, and had acted in some measure as pioneers of an undertaking, over which they so fatally disputed at a later period. But the traders with China, especially the Portuguese, regarded with the liveliest apprehension the introduction of a missionary work which might, from the intricacy with which religious and political life were interwoven with one another in China, bring about complications of the most serious character, and perhaps end in their exclusion from the Empire. Hardly had Xavier propounded his great plan, when he was met by the resistance and even persecution of Alvarez the resident at Malacca who, though a former friend of the Saint, became the inveterate opponent of his missionary expedition. Harassed and at last worn out by the cruel opposition he had so little expected, the exhausted life of the great missionary fell an easy prey to fever, and he died in December 1552, at the comparatively early age of fifty-five, in the eleventh year of his Indian mission, "*in ipsâ curâ ac meditatione Sinarum,*" as the biographer of his successor writes.* It is necessary to keep in view the determined opposition which the Portuguese exhibited from this

---

* "Trigautii Christianâ Expeditione ap. Sinas, ex P. Matth. Riccii Comment.," p. 136.

early period to every attempt to evangelise the vast Empire to which they had found an access through the concession of the island, or rather peninsula, of Macao, and which they had (as it were) tapped for the purposes of commerce and for the sordid and exclusive objects which have ever characterised their colonial enterprises. For this alone will enable us to solve the difficult historical problems which will unfold themselves in our present narrative. A factory had been established at Macao, whither many priests from Portugal were attracted, with the view of ministering to the needs of the residents, and (if possible) of converting such natives as came in contact with them. The Society of the Jesuits at once directed its attention to so promising a field of labour. After an opening in the work had been made by Father Valignani, and Father Ruggieri had joined him (A.D. 1579), Ricci was called as a colleague to the latter from the mission of India and arrived at Macao in 1582.

To give a sufficient idea of the magnitude and difficulty of the work which was taken up by such efficient labourers, in a narrative so limited in its scope as this is, would be altogether impossible, for it would do a serious injustice to the early labourers in the new mission-field whose course in all its stages, and whose undertaking in all its details as well as in its plan deserves the deepest study.

Nor would our present scope enable us to dwell on the threshold of our narrative long enough to record every event in the history of the mission after the Imperial sanctions had enabled it to extend itself even to the capital. The Fathers of the Society, by mastering the difficulties of the language and overcoming the prejudices of the people, as well as by their mathematical and general attainments, had acquired so great an influence among them that they were admitted to the confidence of the Emperors, and opened to the heads of the nation all the newest discoveries of science. But it is to the method they adopted in teaching Christianity that we desire especially to direct the attention of the reader, as this formed one of the principal charges brought against them in a later day, and was at the same time the real secret of their success during the two centuries of their spiritual reign in China.

Ricci had well prepared the more advanced natives with whom he came in contact for the teaching of Christianity, by cultivating their reason and laying down in their minds the first principles of mathematical knowledge. To this end, he translated Euclid into Chinese, and to the *Literati*, the highest class in the Empire, commended the new faith he was introducing by showing its conformity with the natural law, whose principles were embodied in the works of their philosophers. Guided by his example, the members of the mission built up on the other strong foundation of the unity and attributes of the Deity the entire system of Christian doctrine. And as their method was thus constructive, they did not go out of their way to destroy and discredit the ancient religions which they desired to supplant in order to found Christianity on their ruins. They studied with care and with an impartial judgment all the points of the moral law of the Chinese *Literati* or philosophical sect, and found in the writings of Confucius doctrines so closely resembling the teachings of Christianity, as to be almost identical with them. Ricci observed that the most ancient of the religious systems of the Chinese recognised the unity of the Deity, and that they had not relapsed into those grosser forms of idolatry which most heathen lands had indulged in. He even expresses the pious hope that not a few of the ancient Chinese had been saved through the natural law, " assisted by that special help which God never denies to any one who fulfils it according to his power." *

He affirms—and this the reader is desired to bear in mind, as it forms the germ of the great controversy whose history we have undertaken to

* Trigaut., p. 101.

narrate—that the name of the Deity in Chinese is either "the King of Heaven" or "Heaven and Earth." He shows that the sect of the *Literates*, the highest among the Chinese, maintained a moral doctrine very closely conformed to that of Christianity, and that even the great precept of the Gospel to "do unto others as we would they should do unto us," is laid down in their preceptive teaching.*

Pursuing his Chinese studies with all the ardour with which he had entered upon his mission, Ricci obtained at last so great a reputation of learning that he was elevated to a high social rank, while two of his brethren were advanced to the degree of the Doctorate. The sect of the *Literati* and the followers of Confucius were thus attracted to Christianity, and were so far reconciled to its teachings as to become great friends of the missionaries, who wisely taught them that the object of the Christian law was to "do away with idols, and to supplement the law of the Literates."

In all this preparatory instruction, Ricci and his companions were working on the missionary lines of St. Paul when he addressed the highly cultured Athenians, and affirmed that the God of the Christians was that unknown God whom they ignorantly worshipped.

* Ibid., p. 105.

## FATHER MATTEO RICCI

The contrast between the Jesuit and the Franciscan missionaries (who were their chief opponents in China), may be well seen in the kind of teaching by which the latter commended the doctrine of Christ to the heathen Queen Zingha and her people in Angola, where the multiplication of crucifixes and images of the Virgin take the place of the solid teaching of the doctrines of the Gospel, and a sentimental piety is preferred to a reasonable conviction.* Nor less to be commended was the respect and consideration shown towards the professors of the ancient faith, and the desire to learn from themselves the true nature of their doctrines, with the prudent design of showing the reasonableness of Christianity and its adaptiveness to every race of mankind. This naturally drew forth that sympathy with the missionaries which was exhibited by the Emperor and his Court, and which gave them so firm a footing in the Empire, a result which could not otherwise have been secured. When we consider the intolerance shown by Christians, not only to every religion but their own, but even to every form of Christian faith which is not identical with their own, one cannot but feel humiliated at the thought that the greatest heathen Empire in the world presented a picture of toleration, even in the sixteenth cen-

* "La Conversione della Regina Singa dal P. F. M. Gioja" (Nap. 1669).

tury, which might put to shame the professors of a purer faith in the nineteenth.

La Bruyère observes on the Siamese Mission to France of his day: "If one were to be sure that the secret motive of the ambassadors was to persuade the very Christian king to renounce Christianity, to permit the Talapoins to enter his kingdom, to penetrate into our houses, to convert our wives, our children, and ourselves—to build pagodas in the middle of our towns, and place in them metal images for adoration—with what ridicule, with what strange contempt should we see such extravagances! And yet we go by sea six thousand miles for the conversion of the Indies, of Siam, of China, and Japan—that is to say, to make serious propositions to these people which cannot but appear to them to be foolish and ridiculous. And yet they support our monks and our priests, they listen to them occasionally, and let them build their churches, and carry on their missions." The introduction of Christianity into China on the ground of a higher civilisation and an advanced intellectual development, enabled the followers of Ricci to escape the censure involved in the words of the caustic essayist.

During the period which extended between 1582 and 1610, which closed the work and the life of the illustrious missionary, the course of the mission flowed on calmly and steadily, the sound discretion of Ricci and his undisputed influence keeping in abeyance the controversies which broke out soon after his death, and which finally wrecked his remarkable work. Probably even during his closing years they had been smouldering, for the differences that sprang up in such bitterness afterwards had found an echo in the Court of Rome, and the question of the Chinese Rites had been thoroughly ventilated there before it came formally before the Congregation of Rites and the Propaganda. From this brief consideration of the controversy in its germ we pass on to its gradual development in the Roman Congregations, until it finally expanded to the dimensions which it reached during the Legation of the Cardinal de Tournon.

## CHAPTER II

#### THE REFERENCE TO THE CONGREGATIONS

During the years which succeeded the death of Ricci and until the first generation of the Jesuit missionaries had passed away, there seem to have been but few differences in regard to the ritual question. In 1645 a reference was made to the Propaganda in regard to the degree of toleration which was to be extended to the ceremonial and political usages of the converts, and a decree was promulgated by Innocent X. with a view to establish a uniformity in the conduct of the mission. Certain inquiries were made by the missionaries which were answered categorically by the Congregation. Most of these have little or no bearing upon the then impending controversy.

Among the most remarkable was the question, "Whether in regard to the frailty of the people, it could be tolerated for the present (*pro nunc*) that Christian magistrates (Gubernatores) may carry a cross hidden under the flowers which were presented at the heathen altars, and secretly worship that, while they are in outward form and appearance worshipping the idol."\* Probably the inquirers had in view the precedent of Naaman, and the apparent acquiescence of Elisha in his taking part with the king in his outward worship.

I am not aware that there is any proof that this criminal duplicity was actually carried out, though it has been generally charged against the Jesuit teachers. The reply was of course in the negative—*nullatenus licere*, &c. The presence of Christians in the idols' temples and the entire worship and sacrifices therein are equally condemned, and also the ancestral worship in which the memories of their progenitors was celebrated; and the tablets which were placed with their names at the altars received a special veneration. The twelfth question which involved this subject is of a greater importance, as for the first time the distinction between political and religious rites is admitted in the reply; while the inquiry suggests the belief that the concessions demanded were rather for the sake of the nobles than of ordinary converts—"*maximè quando defuncti sunt ex Nobilioribus Populi*"†—words which savour more of heathenism than of Christianity. It does not appear from these references to the Congregation that the chief point of the future controversy had then been raised—that, namely, on the proper term to express the Christian Deity.

\* Mem. St.," tom. v. p. 8.  † Ibid., p. 13.

In 1656, the year which opened the pontificate of Alexander VII., a fresh appeal was made to Rome on almost all these questions, as though they were still open ones. And Clement XI. in solving them at a later date admits that the answers had been given in every case *pro re natâ*, and " according to the circumstances of the time— *juxta diversas Apostolicae Sedi expositas circumstantias.*" Hence he adds : " *diversa ante hac emanarunt ejusdem Sedis responsa.*" * A great latitude would appear to be given to the missionaries by these diversities in the responses of their Oracle, and it may well be concluded that every one of them adopted that decision which came nearest to his own practice. The Congregation under Alexander VII. was the first to come to the aid of the Jesuits, by its distinct recognition of the difference between political and religious rites, and its sanction of all ceremonies which could be proved to be of the former kind. It added this still more important concession—" that the Chinese converts should be permitted to perform the ceremonies towards the dead even with the unconverted, (Gentilibus) superstitious objects alone being prohibited; they may also assist in their worship when they are performing superstitious rites, having protested their faith and not being in peril of subversion, and when otherwise they

* " Acta Causæ Rituum " (Rom. 1704), p. 38.

could not avoid hatreds and enmities." This decision was brought about by the Jesuits, as appears by the statement of the Congregation of the Inquisition which approved of it. "Since," it is said, "the missionaries of the Society of Jesus were not heard at that time (A.D. 1645), in the past year (1655) they proposed four questions to the Congregation *de Propagandâ Fide.*" * They thus were able to shelter themselves under the Papal ægis, and to lay the foundations of the most remarkable controversy which has ever arisen in the history of Christian missions.

It does not appear that even yet the controversy upon the name of the Deity had arisen between the Jesuits and their adversaries, and to all appearance the usages of Father Ricci prevailed, at least in the missions of the Society, until the promulgation of the fatal "Mandate" or "Edict of Maigrot, the Bishop of Conon and Vicar-General of the Province of Fo-kien in the Empire of China."

It is alleged, and apparently on good grounds, that the system introduced by Ricci had been carried on by his successors, by the Bishops of Pekin, of Macao, of Ascalon—and by the Franciscan and Dominican Fathers, with the exception of eight Dominicans and a single Franciscan who

* "Mem. St.," tom. v. p. 24.

sided in the controversy with the Bishop of Conon.*

But we are compelled to admit that, though the principles on which the mission of the Society had been conducted were still maintained, the influence with which the great personality of Ricci had directed it, and the genius of Xavier which had inspired it, failed to guide it in its later history. The mantle did not fall on their successors. The skill and the learning still remained, but the mission had become too worldly in its aims, and too subject to the temptations which its singular prosperity had brought with it, to enable the successors of Ricci to carry on his work with the same spirit and to the same end which he had in view, when he entered upon it as the executor of the saintly Xavier. The latitude he had claimed in the treatment of the ceremonies, both religious and political, of the Empire, had not in his day extended to that almost unlimited license which the later missionaries sanctioned, and which provoked the repressive edict of the Bishop of Conon (Maigrot) in his office of Vicar-General of the Province of Fo-kien.

Relying on his supreme authority in China, and regardless of the claims of exemption asserted by the Jesuits for their order, even against legatine visitation, Bishop Maigrot (as Vicar-

* "Lo stato presente della Chiesa Cinese," pref. p. 4.

Apostolic) put forth an edict addressed to all the workers in the mission-field, which placed him in open hostility with all who adhered to the teaching of Ricci and his methods of commending the doctrines of Christianity to the converts in China. The Bishop was without question a man of a very excellent character and very earnest and conscientious, however he may have been imprudent and precipitate in his action on this occasion. But it might have been reasonably supposed that before he issued his edict he would have called together the missionaries of all the three orders, and have taken advantage of their experience and judgment in a matter of such grave importance. Especially we might have expected that on those points which involved a knowledge of the language of the Chinese and of the nature of their religion and its ritual, he would have sought the advice of the Fathers of the Society, and taken advantage of the learning of the Chinese language which they had acquired, and in the knowledge of which (as was afterwards proved) he was himself so deficient. He sets forth in the preamble of his decree the reasons which led him to promulgate it, the chief of these being the great variety of opinion and practice which prevailed among the missionaries, and their frequent appeals to him to make an *interim* solution of the differences which had arisen between them. He alleges that in order to arrive at a just determination of them, he had neglected no evidence whether from Chinese sources or European translations, or from the society of learned men, in order to arrive at the truth. The most learned among the missionaries themselves were, however, strangely passed by altogether, and, as was afterwards proved in his interview with the Emperor, he was scarcely able to translate a single Chinese word, or even to recognise the letters which expressed it. He was equally unable to carry on a conversation with the Emperor and the Mandarins without the aid of an interpreter, and was obliged to admit in reply to the former that he had never read the book of Father Ricci, " On the Law of God; " a work which had been the chief means by which so many Chinese in the earlier days of the mission had been converted to Christianity. "There are two different points," observed a Mandarin to the Bishop, "to be decided in the present dispute— one relates to your Supreme Pontiffs; but the other, which involves the meaning of Chinese words, and our own opinion regarding our ceremonies, this belongs to our great Emperor." *

The Bishop proceeds to recapitulate the heads of difference and to adjudicate upon them.

* Letter of Father Thomas to Card. de Tournon, " Lo stato presente," p. 122.

I. In regard to the name of the Deity he decides that the form *Tien Chu*, the Lord of Heaven, is to be universally adopted, to the exclusion of *Tien*, Heaven, and *Xang-Ti*, Supreme Emperor.
II. He prohibits the tablets which were placed in many of the churches, inscribed "Worship Heaven" (King-Tien).
III. He alleges that the questions proposed to Pope Alexander VII. were not truthful, and therefore that the supposed permission given in regard to the worship of Confucius and of ancestors was not to be relied on.
IV. He prohibits the missionaries from being present at the festivals or sacrifices connected with this worship.
V. He directs that on the tablets in honour of the dead there should only be inscribed the name of the dead person, and in private houses there should be added the true doctrine of the Church in regard to the honour due to the departed.
VI. He condemns the following propositions:
  1. That the Chinese Philosophy, properly understood, has not in it anything contrary to the Christian Law.
  2. That the ancients designed by the name *Tay Kie*, to declare God as the first Cause of all things.

3. That the worship which Confucius assigned to spirits was rather a civil than a religious rite.

4. That the book which the Chinese call *Te King*, is a sum of sound doctrine, both moral and physical.

VII. He warns the missionaries against allowing Chinese books to be read in their schools, inasmuch as they contain atheistic and superstitious matter.*

He closes his edict with the profession that in thus prescribing for the future conduct of the missionaries, he does not condemn their previous action in regard to these points; ending with an appeal to them to promote unity and peace—a too frequent close of documents whose result has rather been the opening of conflicts more violent than those which they are put forth to terminate.

That such was the result of the present edict the reader will readily imagine. The Jesuits, whose learning and skill in every department of science and art had given them an influence with the Emperor and the Mandarins to which no Europeans had ever attained, and to which it is probable that no others will hereafter attain, became conscious that their submission would be

---

* This would seem to exclude even the Chinese works of Ricci himself.

the ruin of all their power and even the destruction of the work of conversion they had hitherto succeeded in building up, and which had had its chief success from the compromises and compliances with the Chinese civil and religious observances which had characterised it.

These were so interwoven in all their system—the civil and religious functions being centred in the Emperor and devolving together to the subordinate authorities—that it was difficult to separate them at any point, and the Jesuit Fathers were led to regard many ceremonies as merely civil institutions, although in truth they represented also the religion of those who observed them. It would appear, however, from the judgment of Ricci as well as from the experience of the later Jesuits, that the highest sect of the Chinese, that of the "Literati," regarded the worship of Confucius and that of ancestors rather as civil than religious observances, and that the learned and higher classes of the Chinese held that *Tien* represented not the material heavens, but the Creator of all things. In any case it must appear that in view of the immense extent of the Empire, and the various meanings which were attached to its religious terminology, the publication of a hard-and-fast edict, sweeping away every difference of opinion or usage in so arbitrary a manner, and without any regard to local considerations, was an act of imprudence and even rashness, and a proof of administrative incapacity unusual among the well-disciplined staff of Roman missionaries. The knowledge of the country which had been acquired by Bishop Maigrot was limited to his own province, and he appears to have had no acquaintance with the northern and more advanced districts of the Empire. But this was a far less fatal disqualification than his perfect ignorance of the language upon whose most important words he had so rashly given judgment.

The scene between the Emperor and himself at a later date presented a sad though amusing picture of his ignorance, and gave a momentary triumph to the Jesuits at the expense of the Church to which, nevertheless, they professed their devoted allegiance. Of the results of this interview the Emperor writes from Tartary to the Mandarin Heschen, in August 1706, in the following terms * :—

"I have ordered to come hither Yen Tam [Bishop Maigrot] to examine him. He knows a little Chinese, but cannot speak so as to be understood, whence he is obliged to have an interpreter. Not only does he not understand the meaning of the books, but is even ignorant of the characters. A man in this Empire who should show such ignorance would not dare to speak in public, and

* "Memorie Storiche," tom. iii. p. 69.

whenever he did so, would move the hearers to laughter. Not understanding the sense of the books, he cannot say what they contain, as he affirms."

Yet it was upon this mere beginner in the study of the language that the Legate at a later period depended for all his knowledge of it, and grounded all his arguments in defence of the summary jurisdiction which he exercised as Vicar-Apostolic over the whole of the Chinese mission-field.

For when the Legate came himself before the Emperor, he referred to the Bishop as perfectly conversant with the language and literature of China. When, however, the Bishop was asked by the Emperor to recite a single passage from the book Suxu, and to explain an inscription of only four letters on a tablet hung on the wall, he was absolutely unable to do it. "Since this was the case," exclaims the Emperor in a mandate addressed to the Bishop himself, "how could Tolo [the Chinese name for the Legate] say to me that you understood perfectly the Chinese sacred books."*

It will appear from these passages that the influence of the Jesuits over the mind of the Emperor was not altogether of the illegitimate nature which their adversaries alleged, but was

* "La Verità e l'Innocenza de' Missionarj della Comp. di Giesù nella China," p. 128.

derived at least in some measure from the learning they had acquired of the language and literature of the Empire, to the knowledge of which the Emperor attached such supreme importance. On the other hand, the strong repugnance with which he regarded the mission of de Tournon, arose from the absolute ignorance of the Bishop upon whose alleged knowledge the Legate, so fatally to his own cause, rested all his acts and carried on his entire mission. But still more fatal to the Bishop even than his ignorance of the language, was his attempt to discredit the moral teaching of Confucius and to prove its incompatibility with the doctrines of Christianity. Hitherto the almost identity of the moral precepts of the two systems had commended to the "Literati" the new religion. Now, in its new aspect as antagonistic to the "grand doctrine," it was regarded by the Emperor as simply blasphemous.

This is a most important preliminary consideration, and one which must be clearly seen in all its bearings before we can form any judgment on the bitter controversy which the edict of Bishop Maigrot, and the Legate's support of it, awakened throughout the entire mission.

# CHAPTER III

### THE APPEAL TO ROME

BISHOP MAIGROT lost no time in transmitting his edict to Rome and appealing to the Pope for his confirmation of it. In order to estimate the feeling of the Court of Rome upon the whole controversy, we must have recourse to a Roman writer of paramount authority on such a subject, the biographer of Clement XI., Cardinal Albano, who, aided by the Abate Polidori, became the historian of his uncle's pontificate :—

"If Clement deserved well of the Churches of Asia for any kind of special benefit, in this fourth year of the century [1704], it was assuredly for the condemnation of the wicked rites involving certain sacrifices derived from gentile superstition, offered to the Heaven, to the Philosopher Confucius, and to the departed ancestors of the Chinese. These the preachers of the Society of Jesus contended could be exercised without injury to the Catholic faith; others, especially the brethren of the order of Friars Preachers, denying and resisting them, as likewise the Vicars-Apostolic and the secular clergy of the mission. The missionaries of the Society declared these rites for the dead, solemnised with a special ceremonial, to have merely a *civil* character; others maintained that they were of a *religious* nature, and proved this by solid reasons and grounds. Nor were there wanting outsiders who held with the Jesuits, while in the Society itself there were some who differed from their brethren. The first to discover to Pope Urban VIII. and to bring before the Apostolic See the pernicious character of these ceremonies was John Baptist Morales, an eminent divine of the order of Friars Preachers. He, after he had devoted many years of the most useful labour to the propagation of the orthodox faith in the Empire of China, and had often been present at these execrable sacrifices with a view to detect them, in order that he might find a remedy for the evil, undertook a long and dangerous journey to Rome. Nor did he bring back any but a favourable reply, which was given in the second year of the pontificate of Innocent X. But shortly after a priest of the Society, Martini, setting forth a new view of the Chinese rites, in the year 1656, a decree was published of Alexander VII. in which not a few points seemed modified (*derogata*). On this account there arose the greatest contentions among the Chinese. . . . In order that the matter in controversy might be made clearer, many grave theologians were sent and commissioned to go hither and thither" (to and from Rome) "and many books written and published. But by far the chief attention paid to the subject was that given to it by the Roman Pontiffs, especially Clement X. and Innocent XII. After the famous edict published by Charles Maigrot, Vicar-Apostolic of Fo-kien, and afterwards Bishop of Conon, against the rites, and upon some words relating to the name of God, the ancient dissensions blazed with greater fury. By command of Clement, a strict judicial investigation was made of the questions in dispute, and the reasons of the disputants were fully discussed before the Cardinals and grave theologians. At length, in December 1704, the Pope himself, after a luminous discourse denouncing the execrable ceremonies and false doctrines by which so many had been deceived, prohibited such rites by a special decree, and forbade the Christians to carry them on, or, induced by the worshippers of idols, to be present at them. To signify the true God the word *Tien-Chu* was approved of, the terms *Tien* and *Xang-ti*, which mean *Heaven* and the *Supreme Emperor*, being prohibited. The hanging up of tablets with the inscription *King-Tien, worship Heaven*, was forbidden in Christian churches. To prevent all collusion in future, the tablets of the departed progenitors with the Chinese inscriptions designating the abode of their spirits, were to be altogether removed.

"The judgment of the Pontiff was divided into seven articles corresponding to the same number of chapters of the edict of the Bishop of Conon, against which all the weapons of his adversaries had been directed. . . . .

"For reasonable causes, the promulgation of this longed-for decree in Rome and Europe had been delayed, though very many had urged its necessity with great energy. But Clement persisted with great determination in his preconceived opinion, for he hoped that the defenders of the Chinese rites, perceiving into what entanglements they had willingly involved themselves, as soon as the Legate reached the Chinese Empire would have yielded to his salutary admonitions, and laid aside their error, lest by a pertinacious resistance they should bring upon them a public condemnation. There were nevertheless some even then who feared that when the Patriarch" (Tournon had the title of Patriarch of Antioch) "promulgated the judgment of the Pope in the most temperate form, many would take offence at it; that the Emperor of China especially, and the Portuguese rousing the minds of the people against the Legate, might inflict upon him the severest evils. Others ridiculed this fear as groundless; but that it was most just the event soon after proved, and that by the most lamentable examples."\*

The more critical reader who examines the "*Acta Causæ Rituum,*" in the authentic form in which they were published at Rome, in conjunction with the edict of Bishop Maigrot, cannot fail to observe that the theologians deputed to assist the Congregation in its inquiry were chosen from the orders who had so long carried on the war against the Jesuits. The Pope added to them, moreover, another Minorite in the person of Franciscus à Leonissâ who had arrived from China in the hottest period of the fray, and whose evidence is specially referred to (p. 13) on the first and most important question, that of the name of the Deity. The authorities referred to in the *Quæsita,* who are very numerous, are of a very miscellaneous and second-hand character; nor does Bishop Maigrot attempt to claim the knowledge of the Chinese language of which he, so unfortunately for his own cause, exhibited his ignorance to the Emperor. In regard to the tablets for the dead, the Congregation was very reticent, fearing that the Holy See might appear to contradict its former decision (p. 37); while the sixth question, in regard to the propositions laid

---

\* " De Vitâ et rebus gestis, Clem. XI.-Pont. Max." (fol.) Urbini, 1727, pp. 126-8.

down by Ricci, which formed the groundwork of the Jesuit teaching, was relegated to the Bishop in order that he might with the assistance of other bishops and missionaries solve it in his own fashion. It can hardly be imagined that the Jesuits would acquiesce in a judgment in which they were condemned unheard, or that they would even preserve the *obsequiosum silentium* which was deemed insufficient to prove the allegiance of the Jansenists but a few years after.

The long delay of the Court of Rome, extending from 1693 to 1701, arose doubtless from the belief that the controversy if left alone would gradually die out; at all events that the Pope would escape coming into collision with an order which none of his predecessors or successors have ever been able successfully to resist. In the year 1701 he appears to have seen for the first time that this Fabian policy could not be safely prolonged. He therefore resolved to appoint a Legate to China whose supreme authority might override all opposition and bring into harmony the discordant teachings of the missionaries. The presence of a Legate on the spot was so obviously the only practical remedy for the state of confusion into which the mission had been thrown by the precipitancy of a bishop whose jurisdiction was of an inferior and doubtful character, that it must appear somewhat strange that such a course was not earlier adopted.  As it was, the appointment, even if it had been made with the greatest forethought and judgment, came too late.  The eight years during which the controversies had been carried on with all the vehemence and asperity which has characterised the warfare of the religious orders in every age of their history, had made reconciliation all but impossible.  Charges of idolatry, of the suppression of the leading doctrines of Christianity, especially the Atonement, had been brought against the Jesuits by their adversaries,* while the charges of ignorance, prepossession, and even Jansenism, were thrown back upon the latter from the other side.

* "La Verità e l'Innocenza," pp. 90, 91.

# CHAPTER IV

### THE CHOICE OF A LEGATE—CHARLES MAILLARD DE TOURNON

THE choice of a fit person for so difficult and complicated a mission was even of greater importance and anxiety than the determination to make the appointment. It must be evident that the indispensable qualifications for the office would be—age, experience, an accurate knowledge of the language, a judicial mind free from all prepossession; and last, but not least, a temper not easily ruffled, and manners in which courtesy and dignity would be equally combined.

Not one of these necessary conditions, except the last, was kept in view by the Pope in his selection of a representative on this occasion.

His eye fell at once on a very young man, of a distinguished family, without any previous experience—without even an elementary knowledge of the languages or customs of the Chinese—prejudiced against the course which had been taken by the Jesuits, and too delicately framed to encounter the difficulties of a position which would have taxed the powers of the strongest constitution and the most skilful diplomatist.

Charles Maillard de Tournon was a younger son of the Marquis de Tournon, a member of the highest nobility of Savoy, whose name in earlier days had adorned not only the military annals of his country but also the Cardinalate. His beautiful and saintly character might well have fitted him for all the higher dignities with which he was crowned in the last days of his truly evangelic life—for his Cardinal's hat, like that of our own illustrious Fisher, was but the presage of a cruel martyrdom, though it was the just reward of a devoted service. The picture which is traced for us in his simple and exquisite letters to his relations and to the members of the Court of Rome, from the period of his selection as the Legate to China until his death in the prison at Macao, enable us to see how natural and almost inevitable was the affection with which the Pope regarded him. Writing to his father from Rome on September 29th, 1701, after describing the disturbed state of the mission to China, he announces that the Pope, having determined to send an "Apostolic Visitor" with legatine powers, had appointed him to this anxious and difficult office, though, in his own view, so little equal to it.

"He has even in view," he continues, "to

create me Patriarch of Antioch and Apostolic Visitor, with the powers of a Legate à Latere throughout these Eastern parts." The perils of a voyage which in that day took nearly two years to accomplish, at first somewhat alarmed him; but the thought that so many for mere sordid interests encountered even greater dangers, made him feel that he was unworthy to be a soldier of Christ if he hesitated at so critical a moment. "I should seem," he writes, "to have on my face the brand of a coward, and to have cut the thread of my predestination, if I opposed myself to the call of God"— a curious expression, but one which indicated a resolution of mind which was the best preparation for so perilous an undertaking. In a letter, written two months after, he exclaims: "O! how holy and glorious is the resolution [of the Pope], and yet how debased by the election of the subject of it who has to bear so great a function! On leaving the Consistory he placed upon me his own rochet, in token of the amplitude of the powers he had invested me with. . . . . The day before, he sent me his own tailor to make me the episcopal robes and the patriarchal cap, which he had himself ordered for me, directing him to put down the account to himself; and more greatly to manifest the fulness of his disposition in regard to this expedition, he designs to consecrate me himself, on St. Thomas' day, on which I shall enter on my thirty-fourth year." He appeals to his father to follow the example of Abraham who cheerfully surrendered his son to the will of God—the son to whose support he looked forward in his old age. "Consider," he adds, "that I am but a miserable sinner who can in nowise help you through my inability, but am rather a cause of continual anxiety to your Excellency and to our house." He then appeals to him on the ground of the great glory which even in a worldly point of view so exalted a ministry would bring to his house, and the means it would give him of doing penance for his sins in his labours and sufferings, and the need of dying for the confession of the Christian, Catholic, and Roman faith."

It would seem from these words that he had some foresight of his future trials and of the persecutions, which only closed in his death, cutting off in its brightest radiance a life of singular beauty and promise.

We pass now from the opening scene of the legation to the account of the voyage which forms the first portion of the continuous relation given in the "Memorie Storiche" (tom. i. p. 167).

This was written by the Legate himself, and gives so graphic and picturesque a description of the scenes through which he passed, and the incidents of a voyage which in that day was an undertaking of no ordinary danger and difficulty, that we might well have been tempted to dwell upon it at great length, if the immediate object of our narrative did not compel us to give only a brief and passing view of it. Its chief interest in relation to our narrative lies in the clear and full view it gives us of the inner life of the writer and of those higher qualities of mind and heart which, had his other qualifications been equal to them, might have made his legation a success instead of a failure. It records from day to day the incidents of the passage from Rome to Teneriffe, which was accomplished in a French frigate of very doubtful seaworthiness, though very grand and bellicose in its outward appearance. From Teneriffe, of which he gives a lively description, the important and perilous portion of the voyage began, during which no land was seen until the vessel reached the Isle of Bourbon. The incidents which happened during the journey and the natural objects which were so new to his eye—the fishes in all their tropical variety, including that called "Requen," a fish of great size which follows ships in order to obtain the remains of food and offal thrown overboard—the birds of dazzling colours and plumage, which fell upon the decks but were incapable of domestication—these are all vividly brought before the eye. The entrance into the region of the slave-trade, then so largely carried on by the Portuguese and Spanish traders, awakens the indignation of the writer: "Il barbaro commercio," as he justly terms it, "della compra de' Neri, indegno per tutte le sue circostanze d'esser esercitato da' Cristiani." He is surprised that no Christian mission had found its way to the scenes of this traffic, which began at the Cape Verde Islands, through which the course of the vessel was directed. It was unable through stress of weather to touch at the Cape, and probably from this cause several accidents happened to the sailors, two of whom were drowned at this period of the voyage. On the Feast of the Corpus Christi he rejoices to find that the preachings of the missionaries have resulted "in the conversion of a heretic and the amendment of many others who were *mal convertiti*," whatever that may mean. A heavy fog prevented their touching at the Mauritius, and when it cleared off they found themselves within view of the first land they had seen, the Isle of Bourbon, then as now a French dependency, but at that time in a state of deplorable poverty and neglect. From thence, sailing towards the Straits of Malacca, they descried two vessels bearing the English flag, and as France was then at war with her neighbours, they hoped to secure a rich treasure. Presently, however, the French flag was substituted for the English and they found that the crew consisted of French subjects, Indians from Pondichery. The vessels were immediately reclaimed by the Governor of Bourbon with their cargo, so that the captors were unable to claim their prize, which from the fact that the vessels were sailing under the English flag (which was a frequent practice in the days of piracy) might otherwise have become the prize of the captor. They were able, however, to recoup themselves by capturing an English vessel laden with merchandise and treasure, one of two which were sailing in company. The richer one escaped, but the other was taken, securing to the captors a sum of 100,000 crowns. Passing the English settlement of Madras (here called Madraspatam), the voyage came to a close at the neighbouring Pondichery, where the missionaries arrived on November 6th, 1703. The mission included twelve persons, two of whom, Andrea Candela and Giov. Battista de Maii, acted as the chaplains, Marcello Angelita as secretary, the Physician Antonio Marchini and the Surgeon Pietro Sigotti officiating as chamberlains of the Legate.

The Jesuits, who had a large establishment at Pondichery, received the missionaries with the warmest manifestations of affection and treated them with the greatest hospitality. "And here," writes the Legate, "we will close our relation, as the voyage itself was closed, by singing the 'Te Deum' on our arrival at the Church of the Fathers of the Society, to render thanks to the Divine Majesty for so many blessings largely vouchsafed to us in the course of this troublesome and lengthy voyage." *

* "Mem. Stor.," tom. i. pp. 167-204.

# CHAPTER V

#### THE RELATION OF SIGNOR ANGELITA OF THE ALLEGED ATTEMPT TO POISON THE LEGATE

THE Canon Giov. Marcello Angelita, "Promoter of the Apostolic Visitation of the Cardinal de Tournon, and eye-witness of the facts he describes," is the author of the second relation contained in the "Memorie Storiche," and the sole authority for the charge which he brings against the Jesuit Fathers of attempting to poison the Legate. This allegation, though it belongs to a later period of our history, may well be anticipated here, as it is in the "Historical Memoirs," inasmuch as it illustrates more than any other incident of the legation the irreconcilable hostility which had arisen between the Legate and his Jesuit adversaries.

The circumstances which led to this extraordinary charge are as follows:—The Cardinal had dined privately at his own apartments, while his domestics and attendants had been entertained by the Fathers at a more suitable repast. For the fare provided for the Legate was only a pigeon, which was stewed and served up with a kind of broth or soup thickened with bread, which we should have termed bread-sauce. When the dinner was over and the guests had retired to their chambers, the alarm was given that the Legate had been seized with a sudden and dangerous illness. From the symptoms, which Angelita has fully described, we cannot but conclude that the attack was a form of cholera, attended with the spasms, rigidity, faintings, and paroxysms characteristic of that terrible disease. The feeble constitution of the Legate and the sudden and extreme changes of the temperature in Northern China were enough to account for the frequent and severe illnesses which rendered his life there a constant martyrdom. In any case, had there been any reasonable ground for the allegation, we should have found the corroboration of it in the contemporary narrative of the Abate Sala, the most trustworthy of the advocates of the Legate, who merely mentions that the suddenness of the illness had occasioned a suspicion of poison. We find no allusion to it in the narrative of the Legate himself, and at a later stage of the controversy no further reference to it appears among the charges and counter-charges which were multiplied with such virulence up to its close. Whatever opinion may be formed of the laxity of Jesuit morality in regard to their treatment of those who oppose their designs, there can be but one in regard to the consummate skill of their diplomacy. That their influence and interests both at Pekin and Rome would be seriously compromised by an act which would have not only been fruitless, but injurious to their cause, must have been as clear to them as it is to the more distant observers of this intricate history. The incident is only important as an illustration of the bitterness of the animosity which was so early awakened between the advocates and the opponents of the Legate, and as a caution against a too ready admission of the evidence given on either side during the heat of the controversy.

Before we proceed to compare the conflicting narratives of the legation, it will be desirable to present as far as possible a view of the entire situation, and of the position of the hostile camps.

At a superficial view of the battlefield—and few have ever attempted to survey it more closely—it might appear that the controversies between the Jesuits and the other orders were limited to the religious and practical questions, which appear so exclusively on the surface of the conflicting narratives, and in the documents emanating from the Court of Rome. They had, however, a political as well as a religious side, and the material interests of the Jesuit Fathers were even more deeply involved in them than those of the mission which formed the pretext of their settlement in China. These temporal interests were again divided by the political claims of nationalities, and at this point the Society was in a manner divided against itself. As the College of Cardinals in its entire history exhibits the conflicts of nationalities—Spanish, French, Italian, and Imperial—so on the present occasion we find French, Portuguese, and other national interests dividing even that most solid and compact of all corporations, the Jesuit Society. The Portuguese who had had for so long a period a fixed settlement in China, and enjoyed the highest privileges of a favoured nation, had a vantage ground which enabled them to exercise an almost supreme authority over the mission-field of the Empire. The French Jesuits, however they might differ from them in doctrine or policy, were compelled to seek their protection and to take a secondary position during the conflicts which preceded the advent of the Legate. The port of Macao, which was the centre of the Portuguese interests and the place from which all their mercantile plans were carried out, became a place of special security to the Jesuits of Portugal, and enabled them to assist in promoting their national policy, which was to exclude the non-Portuguese, and indeed every one who did not make Portugal the channel of his communication with the Empire, from all access to the Imperial Court or trade with its subjects.

The Superior of the Portuguese Jesuits at this time was Father Tommaso Pereyra, whose Procurator was a German, Father Kilian Stumpf, both animated with the bitterest animosity towards the Legate and the members of the legation.

As soon as it appeared probable that an audience of the Emperor would be conceded to the Papal embassy, a sudden friendship is alleged to have sprung up between the French and Portuguese members of the Society, for this "special audience gave them the liveliest apprehensions."*

Father Stumpf had meantime acted as a spy upon the Legate, and that so awkwardly, that, worn by the worry as well as weakened by his increasing malady, he had entreated his persecutor to "let him live in peace, and cease to come to disturb him."

Father Pereyra represented and controlled not only the members of his own order, but the entire Portuguese community at Macao, and his twofold power was so formidable at this time that no one even of the highest rank in the mission ventured to come into conflict with him. "The tumultuous reaction foreseen first in Rome, and

* "Memorie Storiche," tom. i. p. 217.

## THE ATTEMPT TO POISON THE LEGATE

occurring subsequently in China," are the words of the Legate, "was chiefly directed by the Fathers Tommaso Pereyra and Filippo Grimaldi, through the medium of their beloved catechist Lorenzo, chiefly to cast me down from the favour of the Emperor, who has the greatest repugnance to everything of a tumultuous character bringing him into cognisance with these controversies." On referring a complaint against Pereyra to the Vice-Provincial Monteyro in Nankin, his reply to the Legate was that Pereyra was "considered too great a man—that is, too audacious—and, abusing the favour he enjoys, he undertakes things which the others would not have ventured to imagine, relying on the strict bond which connects him with Fathers Ozorio * in Macao, Amaral in Goa, and the Confessor of the King in Lisbon, by which bridle he holds all the other Portuguese, although superior to himself, in subjection." † Nor was this the limit of his power; for his influence with the Emperor left him without a rival at the Court. His knowledge of the Chinese language, as far as such knowledge was possible to a European, and the many intellectual advantages which his order then possessed, gave him an unbounded influence with a prince who regarded, as his

* Of Father Ozorio, Angelita writes: "Che centomila morti non sarebbero bastate per cancellare la decima parte delle iniquità commesse dal P. Ozorio."
† "Mem. Stor.," tom. i. p. 24.

highest title, the headship of the Literary sect or class which represented the highest intelligence in science and art which the Chinese had as yet acquired. It was this knowledge which had secured so vast an influence to Ricci and his colleagues in an earlier day, and it was carried on with equal success by those who came after him, though the moral discipline which was the secret of its power had so fatally degenerated and almost become extinct. For it cannot be denied, and indeed every page of the "Memorie Storiche" bears witness to the fact, that the Jesuit mission had become not only the centre of political intrigues, but of a commercial and even sordid traffic with the ignorant natives, in which the financial skill of the Fathers was more conspicuous than their zeal for the cause of Christianity. It was at this point of their conduct that they came first into direct hostility with the Legate, and that in the person of Father Pereyra himself, as we shall see hereafter.

From the first entrance of the Legate into China he had received from the Emperor marks of regard, and even affection, which raised in him the expectation that his mission would be received with the same high consideration, and that immediate relations with the Papacy would be the ultimate result of his legation. The injurious effects which his naturally feeble constitution had experienced from the change of climate and other external causes, had been painfully augmented by the constant surveillance of his adversaries, which extended even to his domestic life.

His introductory interview with the Emperor took place at Pekin on December 31st, 1705, in the presence of all the Jesuits in that city, both French and Portuguese, among whom Father Pereyra was as usual the most conspicuous. The Legate on this occasion conveyed to the Emperor the salutations of the Pope, and his grateful appreciation of all the kindness and patronage he had accorded to the missionaries. The Emperor replied in a speech of the most gracious character, declaring the ground of his toleration of Christianity, and of his permission to the preachers of it to carry on their labours among his people. He spoke with great admiration of the work and character of the missionaries, whom he had always protected, and even given for a long period a residence in his palace. The Legate observed that during this speech and in the whole course of the interview, Pereyra showed by a variety of approving gestures that the Emperor's address had been dictated by himself, and that the entire scene had been got up rather as an exhibition of the influence of the Fathers than as a complimentary recognition of the Pope or of his representative.

Many influences of a subordinate but not unimportant kind were now working against the Patriarch, all directed and organised by Fathers Pereyra and Grimaldi. The Emperor, besides the heir to the throne, who filled a less prominent part in this history, had an elder son by a concubine, who is called throughout the *Primogenito*, and whose influence with the Emperor was greater even than that of the heir. Pereyra is alleged to have acquired an influence over this prince, of which he availed himself in a most unscrupulous manner, in order to set him against the Patriarch, while he had inspired the mind of the Mandarin Vang, who acted as the medium between the Emperor and the legation with the same sentiments of hostility which, though skilfully dissembled, had a very active and injurious result.

# CHAPTER VI

### THE RELATION OF THE ABATE SALA

HITHERTO we have followed the narratives of the Patriarch himself,* and of his secretary, Angelita. Neither of these, however, are so clear and connected, and neither so impartial, as the relation of the Abate Sala, which fills the eighth volume of the "Memorie Storiche." Although he held a subordinate position in the mission and never appears in the front of the battle, he has the higher qualification of an intelligent looker-on, and though as devoted in his affection to the Patriarch as Angelita, is more unimpassioned and impartial in regard to the Jesuit Fathers. It is to be regretted that their exculpatory narratives are so meagre in regard to the details of the history, and rather dwell upon the controversies than on the facts and incidents arising out of this ill-omened legation. On the former they defend themselves with energy and not without some

---

* The reader will understand that the titles of Patriarch and Legate are used interchangeably, that of Cardinal having been a much later dignity.

degree of success. But in regard to the connected history and its chronology they give but little aid. At some important points, however, we shall be enabled to compare their defence with the indictment which was drawn up against them.

The divisions of the Jesuit forces in Europe and Asia presented at this time a spectacle which is unique in the history of the Society. At the period of the missionary warfare in Asia, a more serious conflict, that with the Jansenists, was being carried on in Europe; and the Jesuits, according to the primary law of their institution, were maintaining there the absolute power of the Pope and his infallibility in matters of fact as well as doctrine. Yet at the very moment when their brethren in Europe were defending the right of the Pope to determine the meaning and intention of a writer who had been dead many years since, in a work of abstruse and technical theology, and were forcing the unhappy Jansenists to declare that certain words meant the very reverse of what they were evidently intended to mean, the Jesuit missionaries in China denied that the Pope had any power or authority whatever in determining the meaning of a single Chinese word. In the "Observations on the Imperial Acts," drawn up in the defence of the Patriarch, their appeal to the Emperor on the question of the Chinese rites, is denounced thus: "Do you perceive? The Supreme Pontiff can err in deciding the controversies on Chinese rites and doctrine, because his infallibility does not extend so far. .... Poor Faith! committed to the hands of a body which believes in China quite another doctrine from that which it preaches in Europe."* The Bull, *Vineam Domini*, which not even the *Obsequiosum silentium* of the Jansenists could satisfy, and which was the great instrument of persecution adopted by the Jesuits against them, is here evidently referred to as placing the European division of the Society in a direct conflict of principle with their brethren in China, who were openly opposing the Papacy on the very ground which the Jansenists were occupying in Europe.

But yet another difficulty stood in the way of the Legate arising out of the ignorance of the Chinese language, which so fatally discredited him in the eyes of the Emperor. He was dependent on Jesuit interpreters, who are accused of mistranslating his words so as to place them before the Emperor in the most unfavourable light, and thus to frustrate all his efforts to come to a friendly understanding on the objects of his mission.† On one accasion, Angelita was obliged

---

\* "Mem. Stor.," tom. iii. p. 148.
† *Ibid.*, tom. viii. p. 49.

to interpose, and inform the Patriarch that Father Pérennin had misrepresented in his translation to a Mandarin the rank and position of a bishop, in the case of Bishop Maigrot (called generally the Bishop of Conon),* and that with the view of lowering him at a Court which was specially tenacious of the privileges and prestige of rank. It is most painful to contemplate the picture here drawn for us, however highly coloured it may be, of a young and saintly man, infirm in health, feeble in constitution, surrounded by spies, not only of a foreign Court but even of his own people, without feeling the truest sympathy and the deepest humiliation. Had he been sent out to exercise his own discretion, as a Legate with plenary authority, unfettered by previous decisions, in order to discover the causes which had led to the schism among the missionaries and to report to the Pope upon them, his task would have been an easy and probably a successful one. As it was, the Pope, in the superstitious belief that the "*Roma locuta est*" would result in the "*Causa finita est*," even in an Empire whose unconverted inhabitants exceeded the whole muster-roll of the Roman Church in number, betrayed the devoted Legate into a life of unceasing persecution and a death in cruel captivity.

The jealousy of the Portuguese authorities to

---

* "Mem. Stor.," tom. viii. p. 75.

admit the exercise in China of any authority that might disturb their own, and their fear lest the religious warfare might lead to the general expulsion of foreigners from the Empire in which they had almost a monopoly of trade, formed a most important factor in the entire history. Every incident in it had a twofold aspect, and involved political as well as religious motives and interests, the preponderating influence of Father Pereyra being derived from both alike.

The Legate, on his arrival at Canton, received a letter from the Bishop of Pekin informing him that the Emperor had appointed Pereyra as the head of all the missionaries, and therefore he was somewhat imprudently led to make the Fathers of the Society in the capital the medium of communicating to the government at Pekin the fact that the Pope had accorded to himself, and not to any other, the headship of the entire body. This demand of the Legate occasioned a difference of opinion and feeling between the French and Portuguese Jesuits, the former wishing to comply with the request of the Patriarch, the latter refusing to give the notification of his arrival. During his stay at Canton (or rather at Macao) the Legate was engaged in the work of his mission, and directed the Vicars-Apostolic to visit their provinces, an order which occasioned a great disturbance among the missionary clergy.

Preparing for his journey to Pekin, he appointed Signor Appiani his interpreter, Angelita his secretary, and Father Candela his chancellor; while the secular members of his suite were Borghese his physician, Sigotti his surgeon, and Marchini, apothecary and chamberlain.

Before he embarked in the vessel provided for him by the Viceroy (Zumtù), he had a return of that illness which had so seriously attacked him in Pondichery, which is described as a "kind of paralysis and convulsion of the nerves" (probably a species of epilepsy), which left him in such a state of prostration when he reached Nankin that he was unable to land. On Dec. 4th he arrived at Pekin, where the intense cold gave a new shock to his already enfeebled frame. The Emperor sent the sons of the Viceroy and three Jesuit Fathers to meet him, one from each of the three houses which had been assigned to the Society in Pekin. He took up his residence at that occupied by the French Jesuits, where his malady increased upon him so seriously as to give him but a very distant hope of an audience with the Emperor, whose attentions and inquiries after his health were frequent and assiduous. On the 27th of the same month the Emperor sent a Mandarin to inquire into his state, informing him that he might frankly communicate with him the nature and object of his mission. He replied through his interpreter that the Pope had sent him to thank his Majesty for the favours he had granted to the missionaries, and to visit the missions ; and further had desired to appoint him as a Superior over all the missionaries, on which grounds he supplicated his Majesty to give him permission to procure a house for his residence in Pekin. The Mandarin, returning to the Legate after the delivery of his message to the Emperor, informed him that his request had been granted, a concession which filled him with the greatest joy, and gave him the hope that his mission would be crowned with a great success. But before the promise of the Emperor could be fully ratified, Father Pereyra, the evil genius of the unfortunate Legate, appeared upon the scene. The Emperor, who was infatuated in his affection for Pereyra, directed him to translate into Chinese the memorial of the Patriarch, and announced to him the fact that he had granted its prayer. To the penetrating eye of the Jesuit this concession presented a twofold danger. It would have ratified the appointment of the Legate as supreme head of the missions, and would have made the residence of a direct representative of the Pope in Pekin permanent, and the legation itself an established institution. He does not appear to have said anything in contravention of the scheme, but to have expressed himself very sufficiently by those outward gestures through which the Chinese as well as the French convey so much more than can be expressed by the most eloquent speech. A shrug of the shoulders, accompanied doubtless by an expression of the face which gave it an emphatic meaning, convinced the Emperor that his favourite regarded the plan with the greatest alarm and aversion, and led him at once to cancel his concession. This sudden change in the mind of the Emperor surprised the Legate greatly, nor could he discover its cause until he heard that Pereyra had been with him, and of the significant shrug of the shoulders, an action which needed no interpreter to explain its meaning. An incident which occurred soon after tended greatly to emphasise it. The surgeon of the legation, Signor Sigotti, having died of dysentery, the Legate desired the Fathers to provide for the corpse a place of sepulture, and to chant the usual offices for the dead at the funeral. With an unaccountable want of feeling, and even decency, they refused to do this, alleging that it was against the custom of the country, nor would they give way until the Legate exercised his authority by commanding their obedience. It is "incredible," writes our author, "what a grievance they made of this order, saying that Monsignore wished to do more honour to a layman than to a priest, and similar puerilities."\*

\* "Mem. Stor.," tom. viii. p. 15.

We now arrive at the first audience with the Emperor, which has already been described from the relation of the secretary Angelita. From that of the Abate Sala, we learn further that the Emperor seemed offended at the idea of a visitor being appointed, when the missionaries were under his own eye, and gave them a character which rendered any visitation unnecessary. But he acceded to the request that a Superior might be appointed over them, with a condition, however, which rendered the permission altogether nugatory; for he required that such a person should have resided many years in China, that he should have practical knowledge of its Court, and other similar qualifications. The Legate replied that the appointment of such a Superior did not belong to him, but to the Pope, to whom he had referred it. The interview ended by the Emperor conferring upon him the unusual honour of giving him the golden cup, out of which he drank, to drink from. The Legate soon found that these empty honours had no practical significance, and were merely designed to conceal with a cloke of outward respect and devotion the object the Fathers had in view from the beginning—viz., the speedy return of the Legate to Europe after an abortive mission.

Scarcely a day now passed away without bringing some new difficulty or complication; and not the least was that which arose out of the gifts which the Emperor had proposed to send to the Pope as tokens of his goodwill and appreciation of the motives which led to the legation to his Court. The Patriarch had destined Signor Mariani to be the bearer of these precious gifts. The Mandarin, who was the intermediary between the Emperor and the Legate, and who was (as we have seen) a devoted friend of the Jesuits, represented to the Emperor that it was desirable to have some second person for such an embassy, lest any misfortune should happen to Mariani during the voyage. Upon this the Emperor appointed Father Bouvet, a French Jesuit, to accompany him to Rome. The precious gifts, however, never reached their destination, for the Emperor, after the controversy had assumed an acute form, recalled them.

Meanwhile the question of the house in Pekin was again raised by the Mandarin Vang, who was a constant visitor of the Legate on the part of the Emperor. He suggested that, if the acquiescence of the Fathers were obtained, the Emperor might comply with the petition. Accordingly they were invited by the Legate to confer with him on the subject. Several declined the invitation, others answered doubtfully, and promised to consider and consult upon it. But Father Pereyra, having again interviewed the

Emperor, brought back the answer that he declined to entertain the petition.

In the beginning of March 1706 a circumstance occurred which had a very important bearing upon the future history of the legation. For the full view of the whole incident we must fall back upon the official documents contained in the second volume of the " Memorie " (pp. 38-59).

" Monsignor the Patriarch and Legate, on his arrival in China, found that the Jesuits had authorised transactions in money altogether of a usurious character, and his zeal induced him at once to apply a prompt remedy. . . . . On finding himself a little recovered from the attack of illness he had had while at the Court, he began to receive visits from the Christians. Many of these, otherwise well-affected towards the Jesuits, declared to his Excellency the scandals occasioned by the Fathers in the matter of usurious contracts. . . . . The denunciation of these contracts began in the month of February. . . . . Among many other Christians to whom these Fathers had lent money, there came one infidel who was the son of the Zum-tù of the two provinces, and who paid the interest honourably according to his contract. But as the Jesuits wanted (I know not why) to call in the capital . . . . the Mandarin, not having the sum ready, prayed the Fathers to wait for three months, after which time he promised to give the entire sum, which he would then receive from his father, and meanwhile had paid the interest according to the contract. But the Jesuits, not allowing him this delay, did to the Mandarin, according to the barbarous custom of China, what the wicked servant in the parable did to his fellow-servant, and treated him with the utmost rigour. .... They sent many of their emissaries to press him, though a man of high station, insulting and threatening to destroy the house that he had given as security and to have his servants bastinadoed. .... A Christian, one of the most respectable in Pekin, moved by this outrage, directed him to the Legate and sent him all the documents relating to the contract." *

The Jesuit advocates preserve almost an entire silence upon this incident. They only complain that their testimony in regard to it was not heard; that they were condemned "*inauditâ Parte*," † and that the Legate claimed to possess full powers to give a judgment without hearing the other side, and threatened in future to exercise it. But Father Pereyra had disputed his entire jurisdiction, and might therefore have well been condemned for contumacy. " It was enough," he affirmed, "to give canonical value to the

* " Mem. Stor.," tom. ii. p. 38.
† " La Veritâ, etc., de Missionar.," p. 69.

contract (*canonizarlo*) to say that he had made it, and that he had professed the fourth vow of his order."\*

The Legate, seeing that the matter was urgent and that the time for vigorous action had arrived, put forth at once a solemn decree annulling the contract entered into by the Fathers Grimaldi and Pereyra; nor this only, but every other in which (as in this case) the interest demanded exceeded that allowed by the Chinese laws. He declared that "such contracts, even if not manifestly usurious, at least tended in the greatest degree towards usury, and were altogether improper and unbecoming to the religious, whom zeal for the propagation of the Faith had led to these countries, and whose conversation among the Gentiles was for preaching to them the Gospel." He therefore suppressed and annulled this and all similar contracts by the Apostolic Authority vested in him, and exhorted the superiors of the orders, actual or future, to fulfil their duty in this matter. The document is dated the 17th of May 1706.

This was, in fact, a declaration of open war against the Fathers of the Society in China, whose implacable enmity against every one who has even thwarted or crossed them in their way to a universal dominion is a proverb in every tongue.

\* "Mem. Stor.," tom. viii. p. 29.

The conflict which had hitherto been veiled in language of caution and diplomatic reserve, now became open and virulent. The Jesuits saw that their power as a trading company, which now unhappily constituted their greatest success, was seriously menaced, and from this time all accommodation between them and the Legate became impossible. A very suggestive note which the Editor of the "Memorie" appends to the decree, gives us an instructive view of the Society in its new character as a trading company. It is derived from a memoir drawn up by themselves.*

"The Jesuits have three houses in Pekin. Every house has virtually a trade of interest (*un commercio usurajo*) to the value of 50 or 60 thousand *taels*. Every *tael* equals at least four pounds (lire) of French money. The interest given in China is ordinarily thirty for a hundred. The Jesuits pretend that they take only twenty-four, or two per cent. every month. It is easy to calculate the profit. The capital of 60,000 *taels* for every house, makes for all taken together the sum of 720,000 lire, and the income about 180,000 lire for the support of twelve poor clergy (*religiosi*). But this profit is nothing in comparison with that which they draw from the commerce in manufactures, wines, clocks, and other industries, by which these Fathers amass enormous treasures,

* "Mem. Stor.," tom. ii. p. 39, *note.*

which render them richer in the Indies than the king of Portugal."

The reserve and even reticence with which they refer to this subject in their defences is well explained by these facts and figures. While the Fathers presented to the Christian world the picture of a religious society devoting their whole influence to the work of converting the heathen, and writing letters and memoirs from China and Japan to draw money for their missions in Europe, to those to whom they were sent they exhibited the other and true side of their character, being seen by them as a trading company, a body of merchant adventurers, in no respect differing from the commercial corporations which were carrying on their more legitimate work in India, China and the neighbouring countries.

The hostility thus openly proclaimed between the Legate and the Fathers soon gave proofs of its increased intensity. On April 21, 1706, a conflict of jurisdiction developed itself between the Bishop of Pekin and Father Grimaldi, who claimed, under the privileges granted to the Jesuits, exemption from the jurisdiction of the ordinary. The Legate demanded of Father Barros an exhibition of the privilege, but received no answer, and their church was closed to the bishop on his visitation. This contumacious resistance was carried on from April till September. On the

29th of the latter month, the Legate, wearied out with such repeated insults to his office, declared the pretended privileges as non-existing and unauthorised, and deprived Father Barros of his title of missionary and of all his other privileges. He had already, on the 18th of May, by a final decree, condemned Fathers Pereyra and Grimaldi for usury, and degraded them from their office as missionaries. The Fathers then had recourse to their Procurator, Father Kilian Stumpf, who presented to the Legate a memorial, full of charges and threats against himself and Signor Appiani, his interpreter. To this the answer was returned, "Pro secundâ vice moneatur Orator, ut verius, cautius, et non captiose scribat."*

The boldness with which the Jesuits resisted the Legate, though he held a delegated authority in the East equal in its practical effect to that of the Pope himself, must seem to the reader to be almost inexplicable. But the distant power of the Papacy was a mere shadow to that which the Jesuits had acquired in China. The lax decree of Alexander VII., which the party of the Legate maintained to have been surreptitiously obtained on the misrepresentations of the Jesuits of that earlier day, furnished them with the strongest weapon of their defence. This decree they fell back upon during the whole controversy, as

* "Mem. Stor.," tom. viii. p. 36.

sanctioning all their proceedings and conduct in regard to the disputed rites. Although the decrees of Innocent X. and Clement XI. had entirely abrogated the earlier decisions of the Propaganda, they ignored these latter altogether. It may be useful here to recapitulate the extraordinary concessions which the Congregation under Alexander VII. in 1656 had made in regard to the disputed rites.

I. In respect to a number of observations forming part of the *jus positivum* of the Church it granted to the missionaries a dispensing power of considerable latitude.

II. It conceded to the Chinese Christians the right to observe all those ceremonies which were merely civil or political, leaving it to them to draw the line.

III. It determined that the ceremonies observed in honour of the dead might be tolerated in their case, even though performed in the company of non-Christians, so long as the superstitious part of them was removed.

IV. It gave permission to the Christians to assist in these ceremonies even when they had a superstitious nature, especially when they made a protestation of their faith, and the fear of its subversion was removed, and when otherwise hatreds and enmities could not be avoided.*

* "Mem. Stor.," tom. v. pp. 19-29.

But these were merely the theoretical grounds on which the Jesuits rested their defence. It had a far more real and practical foundation in the supremacy exercised over the Emperor and Court by Father Pereyra and the Portuguese members of the Society. This, among many other proofs, was evidenced in the message sent by the Emperor to the Legate, forbidding him from speaking evil of the Fathers in his audiences; adding that he desired at any cost to support them, as they had served him so long.* On one occasion he is said to have observed, "A patron has no disposition to see even a dog ill-treated which has amused him in his youth, when it has grown old," † an allusion, as the Legate observed in a letter to Cardinal Paolucci, to the age of Father Pereyra. We have already seen that another and a very potent influence gave an irresistible vantage-ground to Pereyra at this time. He was supreme at Macao, and at the Court of Portugal, and was thus master of the situation at all points. The fear with which he inspired all around him led the aged and timorous bishop of Pekin to communicate his alarm to the Legate, and even to entreat him to cancel his decree against the usurious Fathers. "He had heard from them" (he said) "that if he did not revoke the decree on usury, and give a good

* "Mem. Stor.," tom. viii. p. 40.   † *Ibid.*, tom. i. p. 25.

testimonial to the life and manners of Fathers Grimaldi and Pereyra, and to those of the other Fathers who were at the Court, and promise, moreover, not to make any innovation in regard to the controversies without first consulting the oracle of the Emperor, a terrible persecution would be the infallible result." *

It does not appear that this communication gave any alarm to the Legate, who regarded the Bishop as timid from age and too anxious to retain the comparatively easy post he held near the Court at Pekin.

* "Mem. Stor.," tom. viii. p. 40.

# CHAPTER VII

### SIGNOR APPIANI THE INTERPRETER OF THE LEGATE

ABOUT this time the attacks of the Jesuits which had been concentrated against the Patriarch were extended to Signor Appiani, his interpreter. On the pretext that the Legate had endeavoured to influence certain catechists attached to the French Fathers in regard to the Chinese rites, they prohibited their attendance at the usual Benediction held at the Patriarch's house. This seed of discord was not long without springing up and bearing very poisonous fruit. For the cruel persecutions and captivity of Signor Appiani may be dated from this incident, though he would appear to have filled a very subordinate part in it, having been merely the channel of communication between the catechists and the Patriarch. He had, in fact, rarely seen the Jesuit Fathers or had any intercourse with them. They, however, at once marked him out as one of their bitterest enemies, and the memorial presented by Father Kilian Stumpf included even threats against him.

A beautiful letter of Appiani, written at the close of his truly noble and devoted life, and addressed to his nephews,* gives us a picture of his character which is so touching and truthful, that, even though in its allusions to later events it anticipates our narrative, we cannot but refer to it here.

"Perhaps" (he writes) "you know not or think not that you have an uncle, and a loving uncle, in the Empire of China, an empire with thirteen provinces, every one of them a vast kingdom. The Province of Quam Tum (Canton), which means the spacious East, is larger than all Piedmont and Savoy, and has the sea for its boundary, although it is one of the internal provinces, and over them all a single emperor reigns, without king, or dukes, or marquises, or counts, to have dominion or jurisdiction. Your uncle only desires and prays for you that God may make you great in heaven. Since, however, the Abate Rubbia da Cuneo, arrived at this city of Canton as chaplain of a French ship, has desired me to write you my news in order to take it with him on his return, I thought it well to give you intelligence of myself— of an old man of sixty-six years—in order that you may know that I am still living, but without the hope either of seeing you again, or of living much longer, whether on the ground of my age

* "Mem. Stor.," tom. i. pp. 351-8.

and of the many infirmities contracted during my travels through Syria, Armenia, Persia, India, by sea and by land, in my way to this Empire of China, where I arrived on the 14th of October 1699, or by reason of the many discomforts (*disgusti*) and sufferings endured during the ten years and nine months of my captivity. These were occasioned through my appointment as his interpreter of the Chinese language before the Emperor, by the Lord Cardinal Carlo Tommaso di Tournon of glorious memory, our relative on the side of the Marchioness di Tournon, his cousin—this was in 1705, and my imprisonment on the 23rd of November 1706. The reason of my captivity was that I held firmly for the truth, for religion, and for obedience and fidelity to the Holy See. . . . ." After a recapitulation of the trials and afflictions of the Legate (who was created a cardinal in August 1707), he returns to his own state, and while describing his inability to return to Europe on the ground of his increasing infirmities, adds these words of piety and resignation, which seem to bring us into the very sanctuary of his heart: "May the most holy will of God be done in everything! In all places and countries there is a way to enter Paradise to which alone we ought to aspire, and in all places and countries there are many ways which lead to hell, which we ought much and in the greatest degree to fear.

The one way is Christ, with the doctrine and example He has left us; the other is the world and the devil, and the lusts of the flesh. Let us cling to Him who suffered and died, and rose again for our sake, and to strengthen us in virtue set before us the cross, fleeing from all else, which lasts but a little while and ruins for eternity." Such is the picture artlessly sketched by himself of the pure and gentle spirit against whom the Jesuits were now directing their cruel energies. They have ever been unable to estimate or even to conceive the inherent might of a single soul " carried up by faith high above shame, fear, pleasure, comfort, losses, the grave, and death itself," against even the most terrible and mysterious of human confederacies that the world has ever seen. Such a spirit is able, in the words of the poet:

> "To suffer woes which Hope thinks infinite,
> To forgive wrongs darker than death or night,
> To defy power which seems omnipotent,
> To love and bear, to hope, till hope creates
> From its own wreck the thing it contemplates." *

From these words of brief introduction to the character of one who fills a conspicuous place in this tragic history, we return to the path of our narrative.

On the day following the condemnation of the usurious contract (May 14th) the Legate with

* Shelley, "Prometheus Unbound."

his suite left for the Imperial Baths of Tan-Schian, where the poisoning scene is alleged to have occurred, whose description has been anticipated in the relation of the Secretary Angelita. While there his illness became more and more aggravated. The attentions of the Emperor were now so marked and even officious in their character as to awaken very sinister suspicions in the Patriarch's mind. Besides sending three Jesuits to be his companions, or rather spies on his conduct, he desired that a mandarin should sleep in his apartment, a plan which was naturally attributed to Father Pereyra, the object being to take possession of all the papers and documents of the Legation in case of the death of the Legate.* The act of condemnation of the usurers and the privation of their missionary office would thus have been easily suppressed. But the convalescence of the patient frustrated this design.

Denied all access to the Court, the Legate determined at last to take the dangerous step of addressing the Emperor by means of a written appeal.† After a long exposition of the circumstances connected with the presents designed for the Pope, and of the controversy occasioned by the appointment of Father Bouvet as the colleague of Mariani, and a petition that the Emperor might

---

\* "Mem. Stor.," tom. i. p. 231.
† *Ibid.*, tom. i. p. 233, and ii. p. 47.

declare his pleasure on the matter, the Legate passes on to the larger subject of the intention of the Pope in sending him as his representative, and denounces the influences which had hindered its success. These he at once attributes to the Portuguese in the words: " I am hence moved humbly to represent that the original foundation of the controversies is this, that the Portuguese do not want any one to come hither without passing through Portugal and submitting himself to the laws of that kingdom, from which has arisen the first repugnances (*disgusti*) against the French Fathers, notwithstanding that they are the brethren of the same Society."

Passing over the less important contest which had arisen between the two envoys, which gave the Emperor great umbrage, and led eventually to the withdrawal of the commission from both of them, we are led to rest on the second point of the Legate's petition, which certainly betrayed not only an incredible degree of imprudence, but (as must be reluctantly confessed) no small measure of injustice, not to say even dishonesty. We are told by the Abate Sala that his words were directed solely against Pereyra, and as the Emperor had forbidden him to speak against that Father in his presence, he transferred his complaint to the Portuguese nation, in order at once to conceal and to accomplish his object. Pereyra was the only Portuguese who had expressed the wish to exclude all but his own countrymen from China, and the Legate, by this subterfuge, designed to convey this fact to the Emperor, but, as we are somewhat naïvely told by his apologist, "without intending to do any injury to the Portuguese nation."

The reply of the Emperor to the appeal of the Legate led the latter to believe that, so far as related to the question of the presents, it had not been faithfully translated by the Jesuits, as the difference arose, not from the claims of precedency, but from the original appointment of Mariani by the Emperor himself. The second, and more important subject, he declared that he failed to understand, and asked for further explanations. On the 29th of June the Emperor granted the Legate an audience, in which he petitioned for leave to visit the provinces. This was refused on the ground of his non-residence in China, and of his purpose of shortly returning to Europe. The Emperor referred also to the ill-health of the Legate, which (it was further suggested) would render such extended journeys dangerous to him; but added that he might at any place during his progress, whether in Xangtung, Nankin, Kiansi, or Kuangtung, gather the missionaries together, and, arriving at Canton, could embark for Europe and return to Rome.

The surprise of the Legate was great indeed at this anticipation of his departure from China. He replied that it was his desire to remain in the empire until he was recalled to Rome by the Pope himself. But if his Majesty should command his departure, as the Pope had no other desire than to satisfy the Emperor, he would deem that his obedience to the one would be also an obedience to the other. On this understanding, this fruitless audience was closed.

The arrival of the Bishop of Conon (Maigrot) in Pekin at this moment seemed to make a general flutter among the missionaries, especially among the Jesuit Fathers. Had it occurred earlier and before the ignorance of the Bishop had been so unfortunately proved before the Emperor, it might have greatly strengthened the position of the Legate. "Ah fosse venuto prima che l'averessimo fatto dichiarare ignorante quì in Pekino!" such is the mournful exclamation of the Abate Sala.*

It led, however, to the concession of another audience to the Legate on the part of the Emperor, which occurred on the 30th of June. Before he was admitted to the Imperial presence, the "Primogenito," whose dangerous intrigues against the Legate have been already recorded, called Signor Appiani aside, and interrogated him in regard to the new comer. He understood, he

* "Mem. Stor.," tom. viii. p. 54.

said, that he was *Tiai ovay*, that is, a man of evil report, and able to do all kinds of mischief. Appiani replied that he had never heard any kind of evil of him, and referred him to the Legate, who had not yet been summoned into the Emperor's presence. At this, his last audience, the Emperor explained and qualified his meaning in regard to the return of the Legate to Europe. He did not mean, he said, to limit his residence, which might be extended for two or three years, if he wished. On the day after (July 1st) the Emperor left for Tartary.

At this point of the narrative, our principal guide, the Abate Sala, passes into a somewhat long digression on the character and position of the "Figlio Primogenito" in this history, which will enable us to interpose a chapter on the arguments put forward by the Jesuits in their defence, and which the impartial historian is bound to weigh in an equal balance against the evidence of their adversaries.

# CHAPTER VIII

### THE JESUIT DEFENCE

"*Audi et alteram partem*" is the inexorable rule not less of historical than of judicial inquiry, and in whatever degree we may entertain the universal prejudice against the Jesuits, we ought not to incur the charge they brought against the Legate, of condemning them "*inauditâ parte,*" or of entering upon the history of their Chinese mission, as the Bishop of Ascalon declares him to have entered China, "prèvenu de beaucoup de préjugés et de fausses informations." We have heard the depositions both of the Legate himself and of his devoted friends Angelita and Sala. We will now endeavour to set before the reader the defence of the Fathers of the Society, which for many reasons is a much more difficult task. For, in the first place, we have from them no continuous narrative, and their direct exculpations of themselves are chiefly confined to the disputed doctrines and practices, and to disconnected allusions to the facts presented to us, in numerous letters from members of their own body, and in a series of very remarkable documents derived from the Imperial Archives at Pekin. To these may be added the long and important letter of Father Antonio Thomas, which fills sixty pages of the fourth volume of the collection we have referred to throughout. But none of these documents enable us to follow step by step the course of the controversy as it is developed in the relations of the Abate Sala and of the secretary Angelita.

We must remember, however, that these were written some time after the events, rather as private memoirs than as public historical documents, and that when the members of the Society were scattered in the general persecution, they had no opportunity of drawing up a united defence of themselves, while the peculiar discipline of their order precluded them from meeting in their individual character the charges that had been made against them. In fact, these charges were not published or even formulated at the only period in which they could have been refuted. Else their profound silence in regard to the poisoning accusation would be altogether unaccountable.

Whether the "Diario di Pekino," referred to with such contempt by the advocates of the Legate, gives any defence of the kind we need, the writer is not aware. It is not, however, referred to in the defensive treatises we have cited, and is set aside by the advocates of the Legate as "deriso e discreditato."\*

The principal charges against the Fathers, to meet which they direct all their chief energies, are :

    I. The suppression in their teaching of the doctrines of the Passion and the Atonement.

    II. The attempt to bring the doctrines of Christianity into harmony with those of Confucius.

    III. The attempt to render the sacrifices and rites of the Chinese lawful, by giving them a civil rather than a religious aspect.

    IV. The acceptance of the Imperial definition of the terms and rites in question, instead of the Papal one.

    V. The personal charges of disobedience and even open rebellion against the Legate, and of intriguing with the government in order to frustrate his legation.

I. The first charge, popularly expressed in the complaint that the Jesuits "hid the crucifix from their converts," was met by them with a direct denial. It rested mainly on the absence of the doctrine represented by the Cross, from the work of Father Ricci ("The True Knowledge of the Lord of Heaven"), drawn up for the instruction of the earlier Chinese converts, and to meet the

\* "La Verità," &c., p. 52.

exigencies of the great literary sect, which held most tenaciously to the doctrine of Confucius, and of which the Emperor was the recognised head. This work, they alleged, was limited in its scope to the doctrine of the Unity of the Deity and the divine attributes, and only touched, towards the close, upon the Incarnation, the Resurrection and the Ascension of our Lord. It seemed difficult to account for the fact that the crucifixion was not mentioned in its proper place and order, but here the Jesuits appealed to the example of St. Paul, who before the highly civilised audience at the Areopagus made mention only of the Incarnation and glorification, and not of the humiliation of Christ in the crucifixion. They point to the lesson which St. Ambrose derives from this reserve of the apostle, and which he commends to all who enter upon the work of converting the heathen to the faith of Christ.

"Read the discourse of the Apostle to the Athenians" (writes that great Father), "which (if he had endeavoured immediately to destroy the ceremonies of idolatry) would have been at once rejected by the ears of the Gentiles. He begins from the one God, the creator of the world, saying: 'God, who made the world and all that is therein,' &c. . . . . Then he comes to Christ, whom he rather calls man than God, saying: 'By the man whom He hath ordained, whereof He

hath given assurance unto all men in that He hath raised him from the dead.' . . . . He who treats upon any subject ought to consider the character of his audience lest he is ridiculed before he is heard. For how could the Athenians believe that the Word was made flesh, and conceived by the Holy Ghost of a Virgin, who mocked when they heard of the resurrection of the dead ? " . . . .
"What signifies the order of our faith?" he continues. " Perfection is not looked for in first principles, but from these principles we arrive at perfection. Wherefore, as St. Paul taught the Athenians, by this rule, we ought to adopt the same order in teaching the Gentiles." *

It cannot be denied that there is much to be said both for and against this principle. Yet St. Paul seems himself to be in conflict with it when he declares that he kept back nothing that was " profitable " to his hearers, and makes the sum of his teaching " Christ crucified." The Dominican and Franciscan missionaries had, however, taken these words in too literal a sense, and a missionary of the latter order, on his arrival in China, declared that "he saw nothing but crosses and crucifixes." †
So injurious were the constant representations of them upon cups and other articles of porcelain, that, to prevent their desecration and for the

* "Ambros in Luc.," t. vi. c. ix.
† "Verità e l'Innocenza," &c., p. 93.

honour of the great symbol of our religion, the Viceroy at Canton was obliged to have recourse to the Government to obtain the prohibition of these products of the skill of the converts, which are well known to the collectors of Oriental china, and probably through this prohibition acquired their present rarity.

It is obvious that both the fact of the crucifixion and the doctrine arising out of it may be made so predominant as to overshadow all the great events of which it is the crown and the consummation. Laynez, in the Council of Trent, whose tradition undoubtedly influenced the Society in all its later history, pointed out the necessity of regarding all the works of Christ, from His miraculous birth to His ascension, as one great work of expiation, to which every one of them contributed, though the sufferings of the cross gave at once the completion and the denomination to the great work of the Atonement. But this was not the Franciscan theory, in which the doctrine of the Cross was so developed as to leave but little room for the facts and doctrines which preceded it, and which contribute equally to its wonderful perfection as the last and greatest sacrifice for the redemption of mankind.*

---

\* The alleged appearances of Christ to St. Francis were always of the suffering, not the risen Saviour. One of these was the occasion of the *stigmata* which are always represented in the pictures of the

Furthermore, the Jesuits did not admit the allegations of their adversaries at this point, but gave proofs of their use of the Cross and the Crucifix from the days of Ricci.

II. The attempt to bring the doctrines of Confucius into a certain degree of correspondence with the moral law of Christianity is denounced in unmeasured terms by all the opponents of the Jesuit Fathers. But when we see fully (as we shall do hereafter) the fatal consequences which resulted from the attempts by the party of the Legate to represent the moral doctrine of Confucius as standing in absolute contrast and even in the closest conflict with Christianity, we shall be led rather to regret the extreme imprudence of the opponents of the Jesuits, than to condemn the plan by which they designed to commend Christianity rather as fulfilling an ancient law than destroying it. The "Unknown God" was not set aside by the Apostle as an idol, but rather identified with the one true God in whom we live and move and have our being.

III. The question of the offerings and sacrifices to Confucius and to their departed ancestors is one far more difficult to solve. Ricci, in his account of their doctrine and ritual at this point,

---

saint, and are not allowed in the case of any other visionary. In another, a crucifix is made to speak with the saint.—St. Francisci, Opusc. p. 566.

observes that the practice had no really religious character. They did not believe that the dead could partake of the food and drink thus offered to them, but held that the rite represented the duties and devotion which children should pay to their living parents; that it had, in fact, a moral and social bearing, and thus might be safely tolerated. He suggested that these gifts might, through the influence of Christian teaching, be superseded by offerings for the poor; another proof of the wisdom of his constructive scheme. His conclusion is: "Quoniam in iis nullam Numinis partem agnoscunt, nec ab iis quicquam aut petunt aut sperant, id videtur ab omni sacrilegi cultus scelere alienum, et etiam fortasse ab omni superstitionis labe purum."* It is difficult to arrive at this conclusion, after having viewed the picture of the Confucian sacrifices transmitted to Rome and published by the Abate Fattinelli.†

IV. The fourth charge against the Society was their recurrence to the Emperor, and acceptance of his decision on the meaning of the terms used to express the name of the Deity. The Emperor had replied to the inquiries of the Fathers in regard to all the disputed doctrines as early as 1700, and maintained strenuously that the word Heaven (*Tien*) signified the Lord and Creator of Heaven,

* "Trigautii de Christ. Exped. apud Sinas," p. 104.
† "Apolog. della Risposta," &c., 1710, p. 206.

and not the material heaven. But the obstinacy and pertinacity of the Bishop of Conon in his fatal controversy with the Emperor on August 2nd, 1706, destroyed the last hope of a reconciliation, or even of the continued toleration of the missionaries in China. In the course of this dispute, the Emperor declared in a louder tone than before, and then ordered the words to be given in a written form: "I, the Emperor, in order to instruct you, have declared that *King Tien*, 'Adore the Heaven,' means the same thing as that which you express in your law as *King Tien Chu*, 'Honour the Lord of Heaven.'" The obvious duty as well as the true policy of the missionaries was to accept the Emperor's definition, and to explain to their people that the word *Tien* signified the Lord of Heaven and was equivalent to *Tien Chu*. But here the Papal infallibility was at stake, for the assertion of which the Patriarch put forth all the extraordinary powers of his office. *Roma locuta est*, and whatever the authority or the learning of the Emperor could decree, in the eyes of the Legate and his followers the long controversy was at an end. In the course of the audience granted to the Bishop of Conon the Emperor observed:

"Before Father Ricci and his companions came to China, no one had ever heard talk either of the Incarnation or of the name *Tien Chu* which you give to God, who certainly was not incarnate in this country.* And why had we not the right, before Father Ricci came, to give the name *Tien* to God; and why have we not the power to continue to do so?" In the same audience he declared of the Confucius ceremonial and the ancestor worship what might be alleged by the advocates of the saint worship of the Roman Church. "We honour Confucius as our master, testifying thereby our gratitude for the doctrine he has left us. We do not pray before the Tablets of Confucius or of our ancestors for honour or happiness. These are the three points upon which you contend. If these opinions are not to your taste, consider that you must leave my empire. Those who have already embraced your religion, perceiving the perpetual conflicts that reign amongst you, begin to doubt its truth, and the others are rendered every day less disposed to embrace it. For myself, I consider you to be persons who are come to China, not to found or to establish your religion, but to break it down and destroy it. If it should come to nothing you can only impute it to yourselves." †

The defences of the Jesuits against the personal

---

\* This observation reminds us how hard it must be and (humanly speaking) impossible, for the Chinese to receive the doctrine of the Incarnation, from the absolute contempt with which they regard every other nation or country.

† "Lo stato presente della Cheésa Cinese," pp. 38-41.

charges of the Legate are chiefly comprised in the series of official documents given us in the " *Verità e l'Innocenza de' Missionarii della Compagnia di Giesù*," which is divided thus : *

I. Proofs of the prejudiced mind of the Patriarch.
II. Of the falsity of the statement that the Christians of Pekin had not the tablets of the dead in their houses.
III. The innocence of the Jesuits in regard to the citation of the Bishop of Conon.
IV. Proofs of the ignorance of the Bishop.
V. Documents regarding the Embassy of Mariani and Bouvet.
VI. Testimonials in behalf of the Jesuits of the Bishops of Pekin, Ascalon and others.
VII. The Edict of the Archbishop of Goa asserting his jurisdiction in Macao.
VIII. Documents concerning the reasons of the final decrees of the Emperor.
IX. Letters relating to the patents required by the Emperor (called the *Piao*), and the troubles occasioned thereby to the missionaries.
X. Proofs of the use of the crucifix by them from the time of Ricci downwards.

* " La Verità," &c., pp. 157.

XI. Discrepancies between the Mandate of the Legate and the Decree of Clement XI.

XII. Criticism of the letter of the Legate to the Bishop of Conon.

XIII. Observations on the Bishop's reply.

XIV. On his declaration against the Confucius worship.

XV. And the ceremonies of the Tiao, practised for the dead.

V. It will be readily seen that under none of these heads we could expect to find any evidence to meet the charges of personal animosity and intrigue, which are so carefully recorded by Angelita and Sala, for these depended on tokens and proofs which lay beyond the great subjects of the controversy, and could hardly form the materials for official documents. They were deductions from a long succession of facts apparently trifling, the results of observations which could only be recorded from day to day by those who were marking the progress and following the current of events which developed so rapidly.

On all the main points of the controversy the Jesuit advocates exculpate themselves with their usual subtlety and skill, and, if we give them the same credit for general veracity which we assign to their adversaries, we shall be led to believe that the latter were too ready to turn their suspicions into facts and to credit every rumour against the Society as if it had judicial proof. The evidence of Father Serravalle, who as a Franciscan missionary might be expected to give the strongest testimony against the Jesuits, is here very important and suggestive. In a letter to a member of the Society on June 16th 1707, he writes:

"Here, at Lin-zin-con, I discovered that the suspicions of the Patriarch are very groundless, on whose authority I have spoken very inappropriately in regard to the present matters. It is on this account that I pray you to forgive the transports into which I was led at Siganfu. At this present time I am well persuaded of the innocence of the Reverend Portuguese Fathers; for in regard to their French brethren I never entertained any suspicion. Thank God, I am very peaceful at heart. I pray that He may give us perfect peace in order that we may carry on the Mission."*

We see here the clear indication of the national as well as religious differences which had arisen between the French and Portuguese in that Society whose every member is supposed by the law of its existence to be in the hand of the General of his order "*tanquam si cadaver esset.*"

* "La Verità," &c., p. 122.

The General, who was in Europe, was, however, unable to direct the more distant automaton, and individual liberty asserted itself in China, as it must do even against the most compact and indissoluble confederacy. In a letter against the proceedings of the Legate, written in French and forming the twelfth number of the exculpatory documents, we find the following summary of the accusations against the Jesuits:*

I. That they had rebelled against the Holy See. This they simply met by declaring that they had obeyed the Decree of Alexander VII., ignoring thus the subsequent decisions of Innocent X. and Clement XI.

II. That they had appealed to heathen tribunals, thus making them the judges of matters of faith. Against this they alleged the claim of the Chinese to be the interpreters of their own language and rites.

III. That they had engaged the Bishop of Conon to make a journey into Tartary in order to ensnare him. This they fully cleared themselves of in the documents we have already referred to.

IV. That they endeavoured to force the Patriarch to write to the Pope calumnious letters against the Bishop of Conon, and this by threats and vexations in order to compel him to write in their favour. This they deny indignantly, and

* "La Verità," &c., p. 157.

declare to be not only contrary to truth, but also to probability.

V. That they were the gaolers of the Bishop during his imprisonment in their house; which they meet with the same absolute denial.

VI. That they had inspired the Emperor with the contempt he had evinced for the Bishop. This has been sufficiently disproved in the account we have given of the origin of this feeling in the Imperial mind.

VII. Lastly, the Jesuits charged their adversaries with representing the Emperor as the persecutor of the Christian religion, and the Bishop as a glorious confessor of Jesus Christ.

Our view of the Jesuit defence would, however, be imperfect were we not to include in our narrative the estimate formed of their course in China by the learned in Europe outside the Roman communion. The great Leibnitz, the representative of the most advanced science and erudition at this period in Europe, published, in 1699, a work called "Novissima Sinica," containing narratives of the highest interest, including the scientific correspondence which passed between himself, Grimaldi and Gerbillon, illustrating the events preceding the Legation of Tournon. The series begins with a relation of events preceding the year 1669, in which the Emperor Xun Chi was succeeded by Cham Hy, then a minor, and under the government of four guardians, who were implacable enemies of the Mission. This relation is from the pen of Suarez, the rector of the Portuguese College of Jesuits in Pekin. The various efforts of the Society to obtain the toleration of Christianity are then recounted, and their unsuccessful result as evidenced in the Imperial decree of 1671. The missionaries, however, were so far tolerated as to be enabled to return to their churches and provinces, where they carried on their work till 1687. At last the relief they had so long struggled to secure was given them, and in 1692 an Imperial edict was promulgated, granting an entire toleration of Christianity throughout the Empire.

This great work was effected by Pereyra and Father Thomas, whose mathematical knowledge and skill in astronomy had given them an influence with the Emperor which the opposing mandarins were unable to resist. The capital was now open to them, and it may be said that Pereyra, Grimaldi and Thomas, had a position assigned them which was altogether new and unique in the Empire. Grimaldi was absent in Rome at this moment; and when the Emperor offered to Pereyra the post of President of the Mathematical Tribunal three years previously, he modestly declined the honour in behalf of Grimaldi, an act of self-denial which so pleased the Emperor that he at once appointed him, in conjunction with Father Anthonius Thomas, to the headship of the Tribunal. Presently a grander and more political office was opened to him, and the Emperor appointed Pereyra one of the three ambassadors to negotiate a treaty of peace with the neighbouring Tartar tribes, his own uncle and a prince named Sosanus being associated with him in the legation. He further desired him to take one of the Pekin Fathers as an associate, and Pereyra accordingly selected Father Gerbillon as his companion. We see therefore how early a close alliance was formed between the four members of the Society we have mentioned, and how inseparably they were united in rebuilding the great missionary work which had been suspended during the persecutions which followed the death of Ricci. Their difficult mission was crowned with such complete success, through the skilful diplomacy of Pereyra, that the Emperor became more than ever attached to him, and the influence of the missionaries became unbounded. Pereyra instructed the natives in music and other arts. Gerbillon, in conjunction with Father Bouvet, translated Euclid and other mathematical works into Chinese. Thomas taught them algebra, and the Emperor loaded them with honours and privileges such as no other foreigner had ever acquired, and none had even imagined possible to fall to the lot of a European. Meantime another very cruel persecution had set in against the Christians in the province of Che-Kiam, and Pereyra had again to appeal for protection and relief to the Emperor, who finally, on March 22nd, 1692, issued the edict of entire toleration, promulgated at Pekin in that year, signed by the two simple words, or rather characters, which declare the Imperial will, "I assent to the decree."

The devotion of the new Emperor to science is illustrated by an interesting relation which follows, in which the labours of Father Ferdinand Verbiest are recounted, and his instruction of the Emperor in arithmetic, trigonometry, geometry, and other branches of science, is fully described. The good Father expresses, in conclusion, the pious hope that the study of the stars may lead his pupil to the knowledge of their Creator—another indication of the plan which the earlier missionaries had so wisely adopted in order to lay a solid foundation for their Christian teaching. An interesting letter from Father Grimaldi to Leibnitz exhibits him in a far more favourable light than that which falls upon him in the pages of the "Memorie Storiche," while the brief but important collection of contemporary documents closes with extracts from the letters of Fathers Thomas and Gerbillon, and a singularly interesting narrative of a journey from Moscow to Pekin communicated by a German attaché to the Russian Embassy to China. The great German philosopher had met Grimaldi in Rome, and heard from him a full account of the progress of the Chinese Mission, and the admirable qualities of the Emperor. He gave his fullest approval to the plan which the Jesuits had adopted in laying the foundations of Christianity among the Chinese, and closes a most interesting preface with the words: "God grant that our joy in this behalf may be solid and permanent, and that it may be undisturbed by the imprudent zeal or internal dissensions of men engaged in the Apostolic office, or by the evil examples of our own people": a threefold danger, alas! too soon realised.

Now, when we weigh the impartial and really historic documents here described in an even balance against the statements of the advocates of the Cardinal, we cannot but feel that even Pereyra and Grimaldi had some reason for the violent resistance which they gave to the Papal intervention. They had been the founders and the architects of the greatest missionary work which the world till then had seen. By the most consummate prudence and skilful diplomacy, they had opened to the Western world an Empire which had been hitherto closed against every explorer. The method they had adopted had succeeded beyond their most sanguine expectations. And now their life's work was to be suddenly broken down and destroyed. It was to become like the ill-fated Port Royal des Champs, not only levelled to the ground, but the very ground ploughed up, by Dominican and Franciscan rivals who were absolutely unable to estimate or even to comprehend the plan upon which the building was laid out. The conduct of Pereyra, Grimaldi, and Gerbillon during the events which followed was indefensible, but it was not altogether inexplicable. They had triumphed over all their adversaries in China, and had outlived their cruel persecutions, and now they were to surrender all their conquests and all their vantage-ground at the bidding of a tribunal sitting thousands of miles from the scene of their labours, and absolutely ignorant of the country and people for whom it was legislating. Surely we cannot fail to admit that even in their bitter hostility there were "extenuating circumstances," and that the three Jesuits who were so seriously incriminated were not so desperately wicked as they are painted by their adversaries. From this attempt to save ourselves from the charge of condemning the Jesuits "*inauditâ parte,*" we will return to the path of our narrative.

# CHAPTER IX

### THE IMPERIAL DECREE

WE left the Abate Sala's relation at the point when he was entering upon a digression on the life and character of the "Primogenito," who is so called in order to distinguish him from the heir to the throne, who is designated as the *Figlio Erede*. The former had an influence of an extraordinary character over the Emperor, who regarded him as "prudent, wise, and of the highest capacity." He is alleged to have been at the first most favourably disposed towards the Patriarch, and to have been interested in European products and manufactures, especially in a certain kind of glass made in an opaque form (*fatti a forma di pietra venturina*). The Legate proposed to offer him a specimen of this manufacture, but through some awkwardness in bringing the wish to his notice (which Sala attributes to the Jesuits) the prince took offence, and the present was not transmitted. The account, however, given us by the Jesuits, represents the prince as being "very little favourable to Christians, and taking against the new missionaries, who were charged with doing many things which the older missionaries had concealed from the Emperor," whose mind he inspired with his own suspicions, and whom he persuaded to institute a judicial inquiry in regard to the whole subject. It is probable that both these counter-representations may have a common element of truth. The fascination which a man of singular personal graces of character—a new-comer, moreover, out of Europe, with all its latest intelligence both on political and artistic questions—might exercise upon the prince, is very credible. But his hostility to the new religion may not have been less intense though hidden under great outward courtesy. In any case, this animosity was brought into great prominence by a most unfortunate incident which did more to wreck the entire mission than anything which either the Legate or the Jesuits could possibly effect. At this point there is a certain degree of agreement between the contending parties.

Among the Christian missionaries there was one who by his mechanical skill, especially in the matter of clocks, had secured the patronage of the Emperor and the Primogenito, and was taken by the latter with him into Tartary for the exercise of his skill in this department. This was a Signor Guety, or Guetti, belonging to the Mission of the Propaganda, and not a member of any of the religious orders. He was a Frenchman, and had been educated in a French seminary with a view to his employment in the Chinese mission. Though skilled in mechanical work, which led to his patronage by the Court, he is admitted by both parties to have been a man of singular weakness of character, very imprudent in speech, and a danger rather to his friends than to his enemies. The Emperor and the Primogenito, discovering the weakness of his nature and his readiness to communicate all he knew in regard to the mission, interrogated him upon the subject, finding that the Bishop of Conon had sent letters through him to Borghese, the Legate's physician, who followed the Emperor into Tartary. His untruthfulness and equivocation in regard to these letters, which he admitted afterwards in a formal confession, awakened the suspicions of his interrogators, and they forced him by a long series of persecutions to confess a number of things which the Jesuits declare he ought rather to have concealed (*cose che havrebbe dovuto ascondere* \*). In a solemn protest he wrote afterwards, he attributes the many revelations he had made in regard to the Jesuits, and the objects of the Legation of the Patriarch, to the terrorism to which he had been exposed by the Primogenito, and which rendered him incapable of knowing or remembering what

\* "Lo Stato Presente," p. 52.

he had said. In his first confession he owned to having made eleven charges against the Jesuits, which he seems afterwards to have withdrawn. He alleges as a reason for his so doing, his belief that they were the agents and promoters of all his troubles. "Believing," he writes in his second protest, "that the Jesuits were those who were occasioning these vexations, I did not contain myself, and I gave loose to my tongue inconsiderately. I said that the Jesuits wished to be patrons wherever they went, that they sought to rule and govern other Europeans or missionaries, that they disobeyed the Pope and the regulations of the Patriarch." \*

Yet in the terrible trials he was passing through, and when they were at the very climax, he was informed by the surgeon Paramino that Fathers Pereyra and Barros had interceded with the Primogenito for him; and this good Samaritan, who ventured to visit him in his tent to console him, contrary to the prohibition of the Emperor, led him to hope that all would end well. In the matter of one of the letters intrusted to him for delivery, he admitted that he had opened it, and had told lies in his attempt to conceal his error. The Legate, in his fifth letter to Cardinal Paolucci, makes mention of Guety and his persecutions, and describes him as "of exemplary life, but supplying

\* "Mem. Stor.," tom. ii. p. 9.

his want of learning by a docile disposition." This docility, or rather moral weakness, was almost as injurious to the Jesuits as it was to the Patriarch, for the reticence of the former in regard to the objects of the Legation, led to the conviction that they were in some degree compromised in its results. The history of the incident, given us by the Abate Sala, is fuller than either that of the Jesuits or the Legate, and was most probably derived from Guety himself or from the physician Borghese.* This version of the story may be thus briefly told. Guety had received a letter from the Bishop of Conon, from Pekin, in which he alleged that the Jesuits designed to prevent his remaining at the Court, and said that he had kept it in a trunk with a view to destroy it. The Primogenito, whom the Emperor had made the judge in all cases between Europeans, commanded Guety to show him this letter. His equivocations and the confusion he showed on the subject exasperated the prince, and but for the intervention of the Jesuits, he would have been bastinadoed. In addition to his disclosures concerning the relations of the Patriarch with the Jesuits, the prisoner made mention of the names of several missionaries, among them that of Signor Mezzafalce, a man of quiet life, and who had not yet been entangled in the maze of political and religious intrigue. The

* "Mem. Stor.," tom. viii. pp. 92–103.

sequel of this unfortunate incident is told us briefly by the Jesuits themselves in these words : * "It is true that the Primogenito had a great hand in this affair, whose results were so deplorable. .... For suspecting that (as Guetti had deposed) the new missionaries would do many things which the old missionaries had studiously concealed from his Majesty, he inspired with his suspicions the mind of his father the Emperor, and persuaded him that it was expedient to hold a judicial examination of the Chinese who were cognisant of the matter." He then ordered the apprehension of the catechist Chin-Sieu, who had acted as Chinese secretary of the Patriarch under Appiani, and of two other Chinese, Pietro Voang and Tomaso Cou, who were known to be often at the Patriarch's house, both alleged to be great impostors. The catechist, in order to clear himself, cast upon Appiani all that the Patriarch had written, and his answers were unsatisfactory to the Court. Pietro Voang described the schism and tumults which had been excited in the province of Fokien by the edict of the Bishop of Conon, and the appeal of fifty of the Christians to the Bishop of Macao against it.

The Emperor, having seen these depositions, was greatly surprised and disgusted ; and the prince and his two assessors, seeing his angry disposition,

* "Lo Stato Presente," p. 55.

asked his permission to remove the Bishop from the house of the Jesuits and consign him as a prisoner (*carico di catene*) to the Criminal Tribunal to be there judged. They demanded also that Appiani should be summoned to Pekin to answer to divers accusations. But the Emperor, on reflection, would not consent to the use of such ill treatment of the Bishop, especially as the two graduates from Fokien who were to give evidence in regard to the tumults there had not arrived. As far as related to Signor Appiani, a mandarin criminal officer was expedited immediately to take him prisoner and bring him to Pekin with all diligence, which was accomplished. A few days after Signor Mezzafalce arrived there, who was not permitted to lodge in any of the three houses of the Jesuits, but was consigned to the care of an official of the Court, with a prohibition of speaking with any European. He was interrogated at the tribunal, Father Parrenin acting as his interpreter, and assisting him as far as he could in this conjuncture. His replies were wise and modest, and it was believed that he would be sent back to his church in liberty. But when he was asked the crucial question whether he held the doctrine of the Bishop on the Chinese books and practices, he replied that he could neither approve or condemn it. So evasive an answer greatly displeased the Emperor, and it was probably on this account that he was included in the edict of exile.

The graduates from Fokien arrived soon after. Their depositions merely proved that the Bishop had opposed the use of *Tien* for *Tien-Chu*, and the observance of the Chinese rites. Signor Guetti, being interrogated by the Court, confirmed the evidence of the two graduates. The last of the accused to arrive at Pekin was Signor Appiani. He was lodged in a private place of detention, and not in the public prison. As the Jesuits were unable to have access to him, they assisted him through their dependents as well as they could, and even went in a body to the palace to pray that his chains might be removed, and that he might be transferred to one of their three houses. But their entreaties were unheeded, and all that they could obtain was the order that the process should not be prolonged.

On the 12th of December 1706, the Bishop of Conon was cited before the judges. The "Primogenito," as before, exhibited his animosity towards the missionaries by proposing that he should be put in chains, and even subjected to torture. Again the Emperor's tolerant influence overruled the cruel suggestion, and the examination of the Bishop, which rather resembled an argument between the judges and the accused, proceeded. His ignorance and incompetence, his precipitancy in not waiting for the reply of the Pope to his appeal, the *lèse-majesté* he had committed in not submitting to the Emperor's judgment in a matter in which he was supreme—all these charges were urged against him with considerable force. The unfortunate Bishop could only appeal to the authority of the Pope and to his own episcopal jurisdiction, and after a vain attempt to induce him to submit to the Imperial declarations he was dismissed.

On the third day Appiani was brought before the Court. He replied with moderation to his accusers. It was charged against him that he had excited disturbances in Suchuen, for which he had been expelled the province by the Mandarins.

On the 15th of December the Emperor, who had been in the country, having been duly informed of the course of the inquiry, determined to return to Pekin in order to bring it to a close in his own presence, and commanded the Fathers, who had followed him in order to intercede for the prisoners, to return thither also. On the 16th and 17th, in the presence of the Prince and the two assessors, he pronounced the definitive sentence, which in substance was as follows :

1. "The Bishop of Conon, Mezzafalce and Guety are to be exiled from the Empire as turbulent and disorderly men ; 2, No European is to be allowed to remain in China unless he obtains letters

patent from his Majesty; 3, All who come afterwards must present themselves at Pekin for the said letters." The Jesuits were charged to make this decree known to the other missionaries. This they did with great expressions of grief, which their adversaries held to be merely the crown and consummation of their cruelty and hypocrisy. But it is difficult to believe that their brief summary of the process does not fairly represent it, or that the statements of the Legate, writing at great distance, should be preferred to those of the Jesuits written at the time and on the spot.

None other of those who were present has given us an account of these proceedings, and we have no reasonable ground for preferring the evidence of one party to that of another in a case which involves such irreconcilable differences and even direct contradictions. If, however, we bear in memory the attacks of the Jesuits against Signor Appiani, we shall be scarcely able to believe in the sincerity of their advocacy of him at this crisis; unless it was an act of repentance and atonement for the unjust charges they had brought against him through Father Kilian Stumpf. The Legate, in his fourth letter to Cardinal Paolucci, gives the following brief account of what may be termed the closing scene of this mission:

"Pursuing my journey from Pekin along the

river to the pass of Tartarugo (I heard that) Signor Guetti was examined very severely (*di mala maniera*) in Tartary. Signor Mezzafalce was summoned to the Court. The presents destined for His Holiness were withdrawn. . . . . Three Christians were put in chains at Pekin, and soon after Signor Appiani, in my presence, whose chains I was able to kiss. Signor Mezzafalce was examined on the sole pretext that he was a Vicar Apostolic, and for no other cause or reason, and because he was a man of rectitude, and disliked by the Portuguese Fathers. . . . . The Bishop of Conon was threatened frequently with chains in order to induce him to retract, and then they examined him with severity (*fortiter*) on all the pretended charges of *lèse-majesté*, the gravest of which was that he had written against the Jesuits in defence of the truth, and after many sufferings, endured with apostolic constancy, he was exiled as a turbulent man by a decree of the 17th of December 1706, the very day of my arrival at Nankin." *

From a subsequent letter of the Legate, we find that Appiani was remitted by order to the capital of his province of Suchuen, in order that the Viceroy there might make strict inquiry into his conduct in order to charge him with some crime. "But this inquiry served rather to canonise his

* "Mem. Stor.," tom. i. p. 78.

labours. For after having scrutinised his conduct minutely in the city of his residence, they could not accuse him of anything, unless we should call a meritorious action a fault, which to his honour they made mention of in the process remitted to his Majesty." It appeared from the inquiry thus instituted, that Appiani had lent to a Christian merchant a hundred silver taels for the support of his family. This man, when asked for the repayment of the money, alleged that "all the goods of Christians were held in common, and that therefore he had used the money for his own purposes." The Mandarin, too, naturally believing that the community of property was a necessary Christian doctrine, pronounced a sentence in his favour, and the Viceroy, in his relation to the Emperor, remarked that the judgment was unjust, but that Appiani did not feel aggrieved by it (*non se ne lamentò*). "Perhaps" (continues the Legate) "God designed by this means to make the Emperor aware that not all the missionaries were accustomed to lend money on usury."

## CHAPTER X

### THE LEGATE A PRISONER AT MACAO

WE left the Emperor on his return to Tartary on August 1st, 1706. His annual residence in that part of his Empire extended to four months, and the influences which were brought to bear upon him there, too fatally deepened the impression which had been left on his mind by the affair of Guetti and the course of the Bishop of Conon.

The presence of the Primogenito, whom the Jesuit writers declare to have been bitterly opposed to the entire mission, though the other party declares that he was entirely under the influence of the Fathers, does not appear to have assisted them at this juncture. The Primogenito, they allege, "inspired the Emperor with all his own suspicions," not only in regard to the new missionaries, but also to the old ones.* However this may have been—and neither party was able to give personal testimony on the matter—it was evident that a storm against the entire mission was gathering at a distance, which threatened to

* " Lo Stato Presente," p. 55.

burst out in all its force on the return of the Emperor to Pekin. This took place at the close of November, and on January 25th, 1707, the long-expected decree was published.

It was announced to all the labourers in the mission-field by means of a circular letter, signed by the Rector of the Jesuit College in Pekin and by Father Gerbillon, the Superior of the French Jesuits in China. They begin by expressing their "incredible grief at being compelled to publish the decree given by the Emperor on the occasion of the Bishop of Conon's visit. His Majesty having deigned, with his own mouth, and also in a written form, to explain the true meaning of the Chinese doctrine and letters, the Bishop, refusing to submit to his authority, excited still more against himself and the other missionaries the wrath of the Emperor." This feeling "was increased from two circumstances: the one, the various answers imprudently given by Signor Guetti in Tartary, and subscribed with his own hand, by which many suspicions were awakened against the other missionaries, and which gave occasion to the summons thither of Signor Mezzafalce. The second cause was the evidence of certain Christians, among whom was the well-known Vang Pietro, who, knowing many things about the missionaries, related them, and especially certain acts of the Bishop of Conon some years before in the province of Fokien. This was what led to the imprisonment of Signor Appiani. On this account also the Emperor is offended with us, as though we had concealed from his Majesty the name and deeds of the Bishop and of the rest. For this reason we left nothing unattempted that could tend to mitigate the anger of the Emperor, with many prayers and tears, but could not obtain any other concession than this, that the Bishop and Signor Guetti should not be put in chains or tortured, nor relegated to the Criminal Tribunal to be condemned beyond doubt to death. We have a firm hope that the most Rev. Signor Mezzafalce will be pardoned, and perhaps sent safely back to his church; though (as they say) he displeased the Emperor by declaring, in his replies, that he neither approved or disapproved the decree of the Bishop of Conon, and that his party neither defended or impugned it. However this may be, nothing has so much shocked us as that part of the edict by which all missionaries who desire to remain in China are commanded to obtain the Royal Diploma, in order to be permitted to do so." They then allege that they entreated the Emperor not to allow the publication of the decree in the provinces immediately, but to suspend its operation for a time, in order that the missionaries who desired to remain might be able to present themselves to obtain the diploma. "We offered ourselves as hostages for all the missionaries." "But how do we know" (said the Emperor) "that there are not others in the provinces like the Bishop of Conon, stirring up commotions among the people, and rashly condemning our doctrines and customs although they don't understand them?" Adding much to the same purpose, indicative of his design to "purge his Empire of this sort of foolish and turbulent men." The letter proceeds with the advice: "It will be desirable for those who wish to obtain the Royal Diploma to come to this Court before the end of next June, since the Emperor's habit is to leave for Tartary every year in July, and to reside there for four months."

The letter closes with the repetition of the sympathetic sentiments with which it opens, whose sincerity it is so difficult to gauge. It was written at Pekin on December 30th, 1706.* The test which was presented by the diploma, and which was applied to every missionary by a personal examination conducted by the Primogenito and his subordinates, was simply this:

"Will you teach Christianity after the system and principles laid down by Father Ricci, or according to the definitions of the Bishop of Conon?"

It is difficult to believe in the sentiments of grief and sympathy expressed in this letter, how-

* "Mem. Stor.," tom. viii. p. 123.

ever we may accept the facts it describes. It doubtless conceals much more than it reveals, and suggests more than it expresses.

However this may be, it convinced the Patriarch that the long-threatened danger was now very near, and that the storm which had swept away so many of his supporters would soon gather in all its force over his own head. He resolved, therefore, to stand bravely to meet its approach, and almost as soon as the decree reached him, on January 20th, 1707, put forth a charge to all the missionaries, directing them how they ought to answer when examined for the diploma (called in Chinese, the Piao), and what their replies should be on all the disputed questions. "Monsignor the Patriarch," writes the Abate Sala, "knowing how injurious it would be to the Christian religion to allow such a current of evil to run on without any attempt to stem it, since he knew for certain that the practice of the Fathers had been already condemned, although he had not received the decree .... made a rule for the guidance of the missionaries who wished to present themselves to receive the diploma, in order that their answers to the Emperor might be uniform when they were interrogated on the Chinese rites."\*

Without going into the full details of this charge, we may say that the missionaries were required

\* "Mem. Stor.," tom. viii. p. 128.

to give a distinct negative on all the questions which formed the Imperial test, to abjure all the rites and observances which the Chinese laws enjoined—the sacrifices to Confucius and to their ancestors, the tablets for the dead—and to declare the incompatibility of all these doctrines and practices with the Christian law.

No declaration of war could be more direct, and none more imprudent at the present juncture. Yet the Legate, after he had made it, seemed to rise from his many infirmities into a new life. "It was worthy of observation, that while we saw the Patriarch at the period of the publication of the decree with a countenance so pale that he seemed like a corpse—a clear proof of the struggle that was going on in his spirit, overcoming all the fears of the flesh—after its publication his countenance suddenly assumed an expression of joyfulness, nor was ever again seen in its former state, notwithstanding the many and varied tribulations which he endured afterwards; an evident sign of his constancy in the resolution he had taken to sacrifice his life for the purity of the faith."\*

Our author proceeds in long detail to give a list of the various missionaries, including the Bishops of Macao and Ascalon, who in different forms and with various qualifications appeared

\* "Mem. Stor.," tom. viii. p. 131.

before the authorities to receive the necessary diploma. Our object is, however, rather to follow the Patriarch in his last journey in China, which was also the last journey of his weary and suffering life. On his way to Nankin he was presented with an appeal drawn up by the Bishop of Ascalon against his decree, which he replied to in a letter savouring but little of the modesty which became his age and office. He tells the Bishop that his reasons "merited rather a rebuke than a reply" (*juridicam non merentur responsionem sed animadversionem*). This was on May 27th, 1707.

The Emperor, after the withdrawal of the gifts intended for the Pope from the charge of Mariani and Bouvet, determined on sending two of the Jesuit Fathers on a mission to Rome to bear his complaints and remonstrances against the Legate and his proceedings. He selected for this object the Fathers Barros and Beauvollier, the one a Portuguese, the other a French Jesuit.[*] Until their return he purposed to keep the Patriarch in close but apparently friendly detention at Macao, whither, by an ordinance dated June 30th, 1707, he was accordingly relegated. The respect and attention paid him in the course of his journey were apparently designed to keep him quiet in the interval, and to prevent the

---

[*] "Mem. Stor.," tom. i. p. 241.

discussion of the burning questions which his presence and the exercise of his Legatine powers might occasion.* These he had endeavoured to enforce, even by appeals to the bull *In Coenâ Domini*, which was never received or admitted by any European Power—a sad proof of his legal ignorance and reckless imprudence.

It was without question the arbitrary style he adopted, and the infirmities of temper with which the Jesuits charged him, arising necessarily from his highly nervous constitution, which alienated from him the higher clergy and led to the defection from his ranks of the Bishops of Pekin and Ascalon. But a more important secession, and one which was made upon much more serious grounds, was that of the Bishop of Macao, who had previously been very friendly to him. No one had hitherto disputed the credentials of the Legate, or doubted the full powers he had received from the Pope. The Jesuits only appealed against the Papal decree on the ground that they were bound by an earlier one, and that they were exempt even from Legatine jurisdiction. But now a question arose which needed altogether another solution. The *Jus patronatûs* conferred upon the Portuguese kings by successive Popes was extended over all their possessions in the East, either then, or

* "Mem. Stor.," tom. i. p. 231.

thereafter to be, discovered. By a fundamental law, moreover, and in consequence of this privilege, no bull or document issued by the Pope had any force or authority until it had passed through the Royal Chancery at Lisbon.

Under these circumstances, and in the face of the decree of the Emperor threatening death to those who, remaining in China, refused to follow the plan laid down by Father Ricci, the course of any prudent man was plain and obvious. Any attempt of the Legate to exercise his jurisdiction in a city and among a people whom he had so seriously affronted in his appeal to the Emperor, would not only imperil the lives of those who adhered to him, but also might be attended with serious political dangers. His duty, beyond doubt, was to have remained passive at such a moment, and to consider that, however his Legatine powers may have existed *de jure*, the exercise of them *de facto* was impracticable, and might involve the utter ruin of the mission to which he had already contributed too much.

Of the events which occurred after his arrival at Macao we have several independent narratives. One which, though anonymous, cannot but be attributed from its internal evidence to the secretary Angelita, is given us in the "Memorie Storiche" (tom. i. p. 244); another on the same side, extending to the end of January 1708, by the

Abate Sala (tom. viii., pp. 207-311); and a third, written in defence of the Portuguese authorities at Macao, addressed to the King of Portugal, which is given in the fourth volume of the "Memorie" (pp. 93-145). This is from the pen of Diego de Pinho Teyxeira, the Captain-General of the city.

Before we return to the course of our narrative we may mention that on the 1st of August 1701, the Pope, in order to give a higher sanction to the Legate, who had hitherto held only the rank of a titular Patriarch of Antioch, raised de Tournon to the Cardinalate. Hereafter, therefore, we shall describe him as the Cardinal, a title which the chronological order of the narrative prevented us from anticipating. Don Diego, whose zeal in defence of the *Patronato Regio* of the King of Portugal in his Indian possessions was as fervid as that of the Cardinal for the Holy See, was early apprised by the Viceroy of Portugal in the East Indies, Don Gaetano Mello de Castro, of the proceedings of the Cardinal, both on the coast of Coromandel and in China, in derogation of the royal prerogative. "As soon as I landed in this city" (he writes) "I found out the operations of the Patriarch in this Empire of China." He had already announced these to the King in a former despatch, and dwelt strongly upon his accusation of the Portuguese nation made at the Court of

Pekin. This fatal error followed him up in his exile, and was one of the chief causes contributing to its severity. The Captain-General, on the arrival of the Legate, called together the bishops, clergy, and senate of the city, and warned them against submitting to any order or decree prejudicial to the royal patronage. He then made inquiry through the Provincial of the Jesuits whether he might, without danger to the city on the part of the Imperial authorities, receive any of the Fathers of the order who had come thither by way of Portugal, and being satisfied that no such danger would be incurred, he admitted them. Thus the unfortunate Legate was again brought face to face with his old enemies, from whom he had hoped that his exile would at least remove him. But as far as we are able to trace their history during their detention at Macao, they do not appear to have taken part in the cruel persecution which now threatened the Cardinal, and which seemed to grow more bitter and relentless as the days of his captivity drew on to their tragic close. We see no more of Fathers Pereyra and Grimaldi. Pinto and Bartos take their place, but do not appear to have carried on their work. The question of jurisdiction overshadowed every other, and this lay chiefly between the Legate on the one side and the supporters of the *Patrimonium Regium*, the defenders of the royal prerogative, on the other. These latter rested their opposition on the ground that the appointment and credentials of the Legate had not passed through the Chancery at Lisbon and acquired the royal assent, which they alleged was a claim admitted by the Popes, and granted by several special bulls to the Portuguese Sovereigns. The Cardinal, who believed that no act of the Pope needed any civil sanction, maintained his highest assumptions of power even in the midst of his present humiliations, and the result was a warfare of citations, monitories, counter-monitories, and ecclesiastical censures, culminating at last in excommunications. All these might have been prevented had the Cardinal observed the usual course of an exile in the country which gives him a home, and forborne the assertion of his claims until the deputies sent by the Emperor could bring back the Papal reply. The first conflict was between himself and the Bishop of Macao, supported by the Archbishop of Goa, the Metropolitan of the Portuguese Indies, who remained to the very last the bitter adversary of the Cardinal, and was finally excommunicated by the Pope. The Captain-General tells us that after having in vain endeavoured to urge his own view in regard to the Legatine jurisdiction, the Cardinal replied finally by his vicar that he " was resolved to exercise his jurisdiction, and that, right or wrong, he would absolutely exercise it, because he recognised no superior but His Holiness our Lord the Pope." He demanded a more becoming residence for himself and his household, which was at once granted him, the first which was assigned him being certainly a disgrace to the authorities as well as an affront to himself. But when he pressed for the removal of the guard which was placed over his person, even when he resided at the Franciscan convent, the Captain-General alleged that it was placed there for his protection as a guard of honour, and not for the purpose of custody. This was a mere subterfuge; for the proofs that the Cardinal was in the position of a prisoner were but too manifest and convincing. He was cut off from all correspondence with any but his own household, and no one was allowed to speak to him but by the licence of the captain of his guard, Antonio de Gayo. A still sadder proof occurred soon after of the violence of the Portuguese authorities and the imprudence of the party of the Cardinal. A French missionary priest, by name Hervè, meeting de Gayo in the portal of the Captain-General's house, was asked some question by him, which he declined to answer, "alleging that he could not speak to him without the licence of the Patriarch, to whom alone he owed obedience." A long altercation ensued, and the incident having been aggravated by a series of imprudences, terminated with the arrest of the priest and his confinement in the prison of the Port of Macao. A monitory from the Cardinal was presently issued, ordering the Captain-General " within three hours, which he fixed for the three canonical admonitions, to release him, to withdraw the guard from his own house, to give all other satisfaction required from him, and not to resist his jurisdiction under pain of incurring the excommunications of the bull *In Coenâ Domini.* He commanded me," continues Teyxeira, addressing the King, " within the said fixed term, to appear personally before his tribunal, without reflecting that even if he had the *Placet* of your Majesty to exercise actual jurisdiction in this city, I am nevertheless the governor of it for your Majesty."*

These facts, which are criticised in a series of notes and observations of a very intemperate character, apparently written by Angelita, are in no important point disproved or discredited. They exhibit clearly the infirmity of temper of the Legate, which several of the witnesses describe as having even outward manifestation, and which was one of the most frequent charges brought against him by the Jesuits in China, and repeated by the Captain-General, who assigned many of

* "Mem. Stor.," tom. iv. p. 125.

these untoward circumstances to the "condizione aspra di Mgr. Patriarca."

This disturbed state of mind led him to have recourse to certain Chinese judges or Tangini, through whose intervention he hoped to be able to secure, at least, his full liberty of action. An attempt of this kind naturally provoked a severer degree of surveillance, and awakened increased suspicions in the minds of the authorities. The contest between the Cardinal and the Captain-General ended in the publication by the former of three declaratory schedules, in which he pronounced the sentence of excommunication against the Captain-General, the Auditor Luigi Lopez, Lobo de Gama, military auditor, and the Captain Antonio de Sousa Gayo; while in another he excommunicated the Bishop of Macao —singular exercises of an autocratical power by a man who was himself suffering it in a more effectual form. At this point the relation of Teyxeira closes; and before we fall back upon the narratives of Angelita and the other advocates of the Cardinal, we may again make reference to the "Life of Clement XI.," by his nephew, which gives us the view taken at Rome of the state of affairs in China at this juncture. We must remind the reader, as a preliminary fact, that the distance from China in that day was so insuperable a barrier that not until August 1711, did the Court of Rome have official intelligence of the death of the Cardinal, which took place in June 1710. The Pope actually addressed letters to him in the early part of the first-named month, more than a year after his decease. This may account for the first statements of the biographer, which show an entire ignorance of the decree of the Emperor handing the Cardinal over to the Portuguese authorities :

"Before the letters of the Pope arrived in China, De Tournon was permitted by the Emperor to depart. But since a grievous persecution was raging among the messengers of the Christian law and doctrine who opposed the condemned rites of the Chinese, by the unexpected order of the Prince, in the June of this seventh year, he was led to the city of Macao, in which the Portuguese are rulers, that he might there remain until the storm was quieted. But by far the bitterest outburst of the new tempest was raised against him in the very place which was chosen for his rest, occasioned by Didacus de Pinho Teyxeira, Governor-General, and the other ministers of the King of Portugal; and also by the Bishop of Macao, Johannes de Cazal, who was a Privy Councillor, and Laurentius Gomez, his vicar, who plotted together with secret treachery, having no respect for his person and dignity. .... The house assigned him at Macao was hedged in with a numerous and perpetual guard of soldiery. A little while after, they interdicted their victim, cruelly tormented with discomforts both by day and night, from exercising the full power and jurisdiction of an Apostolic Legate. They published a strict edict, prohibiting all the citizens of Macao from holding any correspondence or converse with him. The same severity they extended to his companions and household. One of these, a priest, grave in manners and eminent in doctrine, they threw into a hideous prison without light, while on many others they inflicted the most cruel stripes. .... Indeed, when first Tournon reached Macao it became manifest that they desired wickedly to destroy the innocent Patriarch by constant imprisonment and sufferings. After he had received the insignia of the Cardinalate, not the least important of those presidents of the Imperial Court and districts whom they call Mandarins, as well as the Portuguese, raged against him still more atrociously. Pretending that he was planning a flight and thinking of a return to Europe, they charged him with a still greater guilt. His house was surrounded with a stricter guard. The means of conveying to him meat and drink and all necessaries were denied him, in order that this most strenuous soldier of Christ might perish from hunger and need. All who obeyed him were considered traitors, and suffered dire punishments and opprobrium. These things, related in clear letters by Tournon, his companions, and other preachers of the Gospel in India and China, Clement also touched upon while writing to and expostulating with King John of Portugal." *

Such was the view taken in Rome of the situation of affairs at Macao. We will now again take up the suspended thread of our narrative from the relation of the Abate Sala, until we arrive at the last scene which is depicted in the pathetic narrative of the Secretary Angelita.

The arrest of the Cardinal in his own house, which speedily followed his final declaration to the Captain-General, that he had resolved to exercise his jurisdiction in the fullest measure and without any restraint, is one of the most striking and dramatic incidents in this long and painful history. The Auditor, representing the highest civil authority, on the receipt of a letter from the Cardinal, protesting against the persecutions of himself and the priest Hervé, and demanding the withdrawal of the guard placed over him, and the immediate release of Hervé—went himself to the Legate's house with a body of armed soldiers, and in the name of the three Estates of the city demanded an audience. Fearing that some sacrilegious outrage would ensue if he admitted them, he ordered the inner doors of the hall to be shut,

* " De Vitâ, etc., Clementis XI.," pp. 168-9.

and answer to be made that he was in the oratory with the missionaries, having determined to surrender himself with the most holy Sacrament in his hands, of which he had held an exposition in his chapel, where he had been also making a brief discourse, animating the missionaries to suffer with patience these unheard-of outrages for the love of Jesus Christ. But the Auditor, impatient of delay, made new demands for admission, saying that if he did not open the doors he would break them down. To prevent this new scandal he replied that, if the Auditor would enter alone, or at most with one companion, he would open the doors; but otherwise he would not admit him. The Auditor entered accordingly with one of his company, Michele Vas de Paceo, secretary of the city. The Legate having put off the robes in which he had been ministering, and clad only in his rochet, received him in his audience chamber, which communicated with the chapel. The Auditor again urged him to forego his claims of jurisdiction, with more pride and imperiousness than before, in the name of the Captain-General; to which the Legate replied that "he would rather renounce a thousand lives, if he had them, than the Apostolic jurisdiction committed to him by His Holiness and the Holy See." And here he took occasion to say, in order to make him understand the reason which prevented still more forcibly his surrender of it: "If I were to demand the Captain-General to give me up his *báton* of command, together with the fortresses of Macao entrusted to him by the King of Portugal, assuredly he would not give them up to me without acquiring the mark of a rebel. And thus, also, I reply that I would rather yield up my life, than surrender the Apostolic jurisdiction entrusted by the Holy See to my fidelity." With these words he broke off the conference, and, accompanying his visitor as far as the door which opened into the hall, the latter proceeded to the horrid design of a formal detention and arrest of his sacred person, commanding the Secretary to record it, and ordering on the part of the Captain-General and the Junta (*i.e.*, the Estates) that the guard should be doubled, and that a second company should be added to it, which was immediately carried out under the orders of the Captain Antonio Souza de Gayo, who also strengthened the wall on the other entrance to the house which looks on the river. The Auditor then gave orders that no one should be permitted to enter or leave the house, except the Chinese purveyor of food. Signor Marcello Angelita, Promotor-Fiscal of the Sacred Apostolic Visitation, protested immediately in the presence of the same Auditor and all the other officials and soldiers, with whom the hall was filled, and who heard in the deepest silence all he said—protested,

I repeat, against the violence and enormous scandal which were involved in this action, declaring that the Auditor and all his accomplices in it had incurred the greater excommunication in virtue of the sacred canons and specially of the Bull "In Cœnâ Domini." He earnestly entreated the Legate to declare the Auditor and all his accomplices in so grave an outrage to be avoided as openly excommunicate.

We cannot but pause for a moment in our narrative, in order to contemplate this extraordinary and highly dramatic scene. It seems to realise to us the earlier mediæval pictures of an imprisoned and helpless ecclesiastic defying the powers of the world by his resolute resistance to arbitrary power, and we cannot wonder that the members of his own Church regarded the Legate as the representative of the great Apostle proclaiming the supreme truth, "We ought to obey God rather than men." To the eyes of those outside the Roman pale it will rather appear like those later assumptions of power in which the temporal jurisdiction was claimed by ecclesiastics against the "powers that be," at a time when every country was assumed to be under the supreme authority of Rome. But to all observers alike the scene is equally picturesque and dramatic. A young slender form clothed in the simplest of the robes of an ecclesiastic, in the feeblest health and with a countenance marked by many lines of premature age, telling in characters too clearly legible that "few and evil had been the days of the years of his life"—this is the central figure. Beside him we see the faithful companion of all his trials, the Secretary Angelita, fired with indignation at the outrage he is witnessing, and boldly denouncing its agents. On the other side we re-recognise the Auditor and the Captain enjoying their brief triumph, and proudly conscious that they are proving the intensity of their loyalty to their King by bringing almost an army of soldiers to guard a single weak and helpless captive. Then an eye falls upon the soldiers who fill the hall—silent in wonder, powerless to defend the victim of this cruel persecution, but evidently giving but grudging aid to those who were directing it against him.* When we remember how mixed was this multitude, how varied their nationality, their appearance, their costume, we may complete the picture in our imagination, and give it the light and shade and variety of colour it presented in the original. The Legate, whose sole arms were monitions and excommunications, could only meet his assailants with these somewhat antiquated weapons—fruitless as those

* "I soldati medesimi . . . . più timorati di Dio che gli ecclesiastici e religiosi moderavano talora quando non v'era presente il Capitano nell'esecuzione il rigore di tali determinazioni."—"Mem. Stor.," tom. i. p. 283.

which the Anti-Popes hurled against one another with so little effect in days when the civil results of spiritual censures made them so additionally formidable. But these cruel persecutions elicited the sympathy even of the higher Chinese officials. The Governor of the district had been desired by the Procurator of the city to remove the Chinese servants of the Legate from their posts. But when he had been duly informed in the matter, he refused to do so, and enjoined them all to serve the Legate faithfully. On a later occasion he made an earnest and friendly appeal to the Procurator to withdraw the guard from the house of the Legate, and to liberate the unfortunate priest Hervé. This was as ineffectual as the monitions of the Legate himself, and the reason was apparent. The question had passed from a mere ecclesiastical one into the domain of politics. The Portuguese interests as traders and the authority of the Government at Lisbon were represented as being in jeopardy. Even the Jesuits, if they had attempted to mediate at such a juncture, would have been powerless. Whatever, therefore, may be set to their account during the residence of the Legate in China, they could not be held responsible for the cruelty of the Portuguese authorities at Macao, where they were themselves living only on sufferance. We cannot, then, fairly impute to any agency other than that of the Captain-General and his satellites, the afflictions of the later days of a prelate who in a feebler frame and with vastly inferior qualifications was imitating the example of Becket in defence of "ecclesiastical liberty."

On July 24th the Bishop of Macao, hitherto friendly to the Legate, published a mandate against obedience to his jurisdiction on four special grounds, which certainly are not without solidity, and may be here briefly indicated:

I. The first claimed exemption from the Legatine visitation on the ground of the *Patrimonio Regio* of the kings of Portugal, which secured the whole of the Indies then or since then to be discovered from the effects of any Papal Bull which had not passed through the Chancery of the kingdom. This exemption was without doubt suggested by Teyxeira.

II. The memorial presented to the Emperor, reflecting on the Portuguese nation and specially against the residents of that nation at Macao.

III. The fact that the Holy See had not been duly informed of the state of affairs in China, and that the Emperor had sent a representation to the Pope which had the force of an appeal, pending which the Legate could not act.

IV. That the edict of the Legate was issued only a few days after the Emperor's decree, to which it was entirely opposed—a course which was contrary to the rule of the Council of Trent (sess. xiv. c. 7).

The publication of this document betrayed the Legate into a new exercise of his excommunicating power. This only occasioned new troubles, which the Abate Sala attributes to the Portuguese alone. " The vexations," he writes, " which the Patriarch received from the Portuguese are indescribable. . . . . But in the midst of so many ills, he had the consolation of being attended by faithful Chinese servants, who most carefully kept all his letters for him, so that only one, which was from Signor Hervé, was lost." Presently a ray of light fell over the scene, and it came from the direction of England. We may well be proud that it was left for a benevolent Englishman, Captain Harrison (called by Sala, Harizon and Arizon), to bring messages and letters of comfort to the Legate, and to pay him all the offices of kindness which had been so rigidly denied him by those of his own country and communion. " This Harrison made entreaty to the Captain-General to be permitted to visit Monsignore, but it was refused. He urged that the course which was being pursued towards him appeared incomprehensible in Europe. The Captain-General replied that it was by order of the Emperor of China that he was so treated, and thought to excuse himself by a palpable falsehood, which only made him the more guilty, as he thus declared himself the minister of a heathen prince against an Apostolic Legate."* The Captain-General, probably induced by the fear of incurring the whole responsibility for these excesses, had called an assembly of the three Estates of the city. Among those who attended were the Bishop of Macao and some of his clergy, including several Franciscans and two Jesuits, the Provincial Father Francesco Pinto and Bastos. He compelled all present to subscribe a document confirming all his acts, including the imprisonment of the Cardinal De Tournon (*obbligò tutti sottoscrivere*). The reason alleged was again the vindication of the *Patrimonio Regio*, which gave the entire persecution a political rather than a religious character. The narrative of Sala now leaves the history of the imprisoned missionaries at Macao to follow up the fortunes of those in China, and describe the application to each of them individually of the test required by the Emperor. We are, therefore, led again to have recourse to the relation of Angelita, the only companion of the Cardinal in his last days and the only recorder of their touching close. This is given in a separate memoir, entitled "Della preziosa morte dell' Eminentiss. e Reverendiss. Carlo Tommaso Maillard de Tournon . . . seguita nella città di Macao gli 8 del mese di Giugno,

* "Mem. Stor.," tom. viii. p. 249.

dell' anno 1710, e di ciò che gli avvenne negli ultimi cinque mesi della sua vita."*

After a brief prelude, the narrator thus proceeds:

"The reason for which the Apostolic Legate was confined by the Emperor of China in the city of Macao is known to all. It was that he had opposed himself with Apostolic zeal to the superstitions of the Chinese rites, not so much by word of mouth to the Mandarins of the Court of Pekin, as in the rule he put forth to the missionaries in the edict published at Nankin on February 7th, 1707. This was the grave offence ascribed to him in one of the interlocutory decrees of the Emperor himself, with the menace, further, of the penalty of death : 'In future, if there are found any among you Europeans who, in preaching your law, contravene the Chinese doctrine, they shall be taken and killed. You, therefore, run as fast as you can after Tolo (the Chinese name for De Tournon), apprise him of these matters, advise him no longer to excite disturbances: for if such things occur again, Tolo shall be apprehended, led hither, and put to death.'"

But the Mandarins explained to the Emperor that, as the Christians held it to be most glorious to die for their faith, it would be better to find some mode of punishment which might bring with

* " Mem. Stor.," tom. i. pp. 294-330.

it dishonour, and prevent their receiving glory from martyrdom. The Emperor therefore adopted another plan to effect his purpose:

"He resolved to send the Legate to Macao, a city lying in a peninsula united to the mainland by a narrow tongue of land which leads to the city of Kuang-Ceu, metropolis of the province of Kuang-tung or Canton. By a convention between the Crown of Portugal and the Emperor of China, the Chinese inhabitants of Macao depend absolutely on the Mandarins of Hian-San-Hien, a city of the third inferior order, while the inhabitants of every other nation are under the full jurisdiction of the King of Portugal, by means of a Governor who has the title of Captain-General."

These facts enable us to explain the frequent passages of the narrative which exhibit a kind of co-ordinate jurisdiction of the Chinese and Portuguese authorities, and the intervention of the Mandarins whenever any question arises between the former and the latter nationalities.

"With the year 1710 the persecution against the Legate had a greater recrudescence. A small frigate arrived at Macao, bringing six missionaries from Manila who were the bearers of the Cardinalitial beretta."

The bestowal of this high dignity on the Legate occasioned a still more bitter hostility against him. An opportunity of exhibiting this occurred soon after. The Legate had given an asylum in his house to four poor missionaries, who were able to enter it from the circumstance that the guard had for some reason been withdrawn by the Captain-General. After having passed through cruel persecutions, they arrived at Macao in so destitute a state that their wretched condition moved the benevolent heart of the Legate, "who could not see them perish miserably in the streets under his own eyes." This act of charity was brought as a heavy charge against him. But far more serious in its results was the suspicion that he was planning an escape, and holding correspondence with the Chinese authorities in order to effect it. No greater insult could have been devised by his bitterest enemy than even the insinuation that a martyr, already, in a manner, tied to the stake, should yield to the last temptation of our mortal weakness—the love of life. His life had been too truly a living death to make him love it for its own sake; and the only fear that he could have at such a moment was that he should leave the mission that was entrusted to him headless and helpless, without a guide and almost without a friend. But here he felt, as every true servant of Christ must feel, and as one of another creed has so well expressed the sentiment :

"I am leaving the ship of the Church in a storm; but whilst the great Pilot is in it the loss of a poor under-rower will be inconsiderable." *

On the arrival of the Cardinalitial insignia, in order to prove to the Emperor the legitimacy of his claims to represent the Pope, and the full recognition by His Holiness of the fidelity with which he had executed his Legatine office, he addressed a letter to him in Chinese, adding a version of it in Italian, and transmitted it by three missionaries who were destined to go to Pekin as instructors in mathematics, music, and painting. Great difficulties were interposed by the Mandarins at Canton to its transmission, and whether it reached the Emperor does not appear from our narrative:

"In the midst of the furious tempest that raged around him, his Eminence resolved to celebrate a solemn function in his chapel for the reception of the beretta. As witnesses of this touching ceremony he invited all the missionaries of the different orders who were then at Macao, and having celebrated the holy Mass, he read the Pontifical brief declaring his promotion, and took the accustomed oath of cardinals on their election. After this he was presented by the eldest of the missionaries with the beretta, which he placed upon his head, and proceeded to chant the Te Deum. Then, standing under the baldachino, he

* Dr. Owen to Ch. Fleetwood, Esq., Aug. 1683.

made a brief discourse to those present, protesting that he recognised this dignity as the fruit of the mission, after which all the missionaries pledged him their obedience, neither the circumstances of place or time permitting a greater solemnity.*

Yet what most solemn function which was ever performed amid the most gorgeous surroundings of Roman ceremonial could have a moral grandeur equal to this touching service—sublime in its very simplicity and intensely impressive from the very circumstances which reduced it to such slender and strange proportions? The prison-scene carries back our thoughts to the Church of the catacombs, to the day of the greatest victories of our faith, when the feeble band of disciples stood helpless and alone to deliver their great testimony for Christ against the world, and the Christian worship was carried on rather in the prison or the crypt than in the splendour of the basilica. Alone in the midst of millions of idolaters—deserted by his own at the moment of his greatest need—the beretta must have seemed rather the representative of the martyr's crown than the symbol of a mere earthly dignity. It was a prophecy of death no less than the Cardinal's hat of the venerable Fisher, and pictured almost the latest of the stations of his cross of prolonged endurance and patient suffering. And never was

* "Mem. Stor.," tom. i. p. 306.

K

cross more bravely and manfully borne than by the feeble hand of the dying Cardinal—never were the words of the older saint more touchingly verified:

> "Charum onus ut Christi leve pondus sumit et adfert
> Tam volucri cursu, tamquam magis ipse feratur
> Nec ferat ; et vere Christus fert ipse ferentem."\*

The rumour that the Cardinal was planning an escape was now spread about with fresh accessories. It was alleged that the vessel from Manila was to supply the means for his flight, and his house was now guarded on every side so strictly that even necessaries of life were being denied him. Fresh water could be no more procured, and the unhappy prisoners were obliged to drink salt water drawn from the well, instead of the clear water of the public fountain. A Mandarin who, for some cause or other, which does not appear, entered with an unusual degree of zeal into the work of persecution, issued an edict commanding all the Chinese servants of the Cardinal to leave within three days. Against this decree, full of calumnies and misrepresentations, the Cardinal appealed to the Viceroy of Canton, who nobly, but, alas! too late, vindicated him against his persecutor. For when his sentence in behalf of the Cardinal was published at Macao, the subject of this long

\* "Paulin. Nolan. Nat." iv.

history of tyranny and outrage had passed away from the scene of his many sorrows.

"It is time now"—we may well make these words of this faithful eye-witness our own—"that we should bring this relation to an end by describing the happy departure of the Cardinal from labour to rest, from the warfare to the crown. Three months before his death he began to feel internal pains, which constantly increased upon him in the same degree as the plots, calumnies, and outrages which his persecutors were every day contriving against him, borne, however, with incredible calmness, indifference, and resignation to the Divine Will. But although his spirit rose high above every sinister event, the weakness of the flesh could no longer resist the internal pains (*si colici, che di ventre*) to which he was at last obliged to yield, and to take to his bed about the 25th of April 1710. This bed was rather his cross than his rest; for he suffered more lying down than standing, and in such a manner that it was necessary for him to pass from one bed to another, sometimes to sit and sometimes to stand. This continued for the space of two months without intermission, both day and night, with great suffering. In the three last weeks of his life the Chinese authorities permitted the new missionaries who came to Macao with the beretta, to come every day to the house to visit him, and it appeared as though the Divine Providence had conducted them thither at such a time, in order that he might have the consolation of finding himself assisted in the last days of his painful life, and at the very point of his precious death, by such good servants of God and obedient ministers of the Apostolic See. On the morning of Sunday, the 8th of June 1710, on the Feast of the most holy Pentecost, all the missionaries hastened early to the house of His Eminence, who, notwithstanding that he was suffering on the neck, the arms, and the legs from the remedies used the night before, resolved to rise from the bed to hear the holy office in his chapel. Before he heard it, he made a sacramental confession, and afterwards, seated on a chair, assisted with great devotion in the divine mystery, celebrated in an alb by Signor Andrea Candela, his chaplain and Chancellor of Visitation. Then he received the most holy Viaticum with the greatest devotion and fervour. When the Mass was ended, he wished on every account to remain to pray before the altar, but, yielding to the prayers of his physician, Domenico Marchini, who thought it necessary for him to take rest, he was brought back to his bed, or, to speak more truly, to his cross. Four hours afterwards he was seized with an attack of apoplexy, on which account he was fortified with the extreme unction, administered by the Father Giuseppe Cerù, one of the new missionaries. In the very act of the recommendation of his soul, while the priest was uttering the second prayer, *Commendo te,* &c., in that very hour in which the Church was celebrating the descent of the Holy Ghost on the Apostles, he rendered up his unconquered spirit to God—having lived forty-one years, five months, and eighteen days. Thus gloriously did this valiant champion of the Church finish the course both of his life and of his warfare." *

It would seem a kind of sacrilege to add a single line to a picture of such exquisite beauty and pathetic interest. But if we cannot add anything to it, we may bring much from it. It sets before us the strength of Christ made perfect in weakness—faith triumphant over every fear and doubt—hope outliving even the wreck of every earthly support—and opens to our hearts the prophecy of that brighter day when the aspirations of Xavier, the labours of Ricci, and the martyred life of Tournon shall bear fruit in the very midst of that great empire in which their word was at first received so gladly, and their work at last so suddenly perished. But we are summoned away from the memories of the parted

---

* "Relazione della preziosa morte del Em. Carlo Tom. Maillard de Tournon."—"Mem. Stor.," tom. i. pp. 317-19.

life, and all its impressive lessons, to a much sadder and more painful retrospect. We are led at the present moment rather to look back upon the causes of this cruel sacrifice of a precious life than to contemplate the mournful result. The question forces itself upon us : " Who, either at Rome, or in China, or Portugal, were really responsible for so irreparable a loss ? How are we to apportion the blame and to measure the liability of any or all of those whom we have already shown to have contributed to the failure of the Cardinal's mission and to his ceaseless persecution and untimely death ?" Our attempt to answer these questions must be left for the following chapter.

# CHAPTER XI.

### THE QUESTION IN REGARD TO THE COURT OF ROME.

CLEMENT XI., best known to the Church and the secular Powers of Europe as the author of the unfortunate Bull *Unigenitus*, and the cruel persecutions of which it was so fruitful a cause, was also, in regard to the troubles of China and all their sad results, the *fons et origo malorum*. We have already seen how fatal an error he committed in selecting for such a mission a saint, instead of a prophet—a young man with every possible disqualification, instead of a man of age and experience, able to treat with emperors as well as with ecclesiastics, conversant with the language and customs of that great empire which was then a real *terra incognita*. But after he had committed so great an error, he was presently involved in political complications which rendered it difficult, if not even impossible, for him to assist with his spiritual or temporal powers the saintly man—little more than a youth—whom he had launched upon so troubled a sea. He was engaged in a conflict with the Jansenists, in which he was too closely allied with the Jesuits to be enabled to attack them successfully in the distant world of China. He was involved at the same time in a serious controversy with the King of Portugal on the tribute of the clergy to the Papacy, which in England is called the "Tenths," in Portugal the "Fifteenths" (*Quindennii*). He was unable, therefore, to act with the boldness of an apostle, and to rebuke, and, if need be, even censure, the King of Portugal for allowing the deeds of his servants in Macao, and was obliged to satisfy his conscience by feeble and querulous appeals during the captivity of the Cardinal, while after his death he charges the King very plainly with having been the chief cause of it. "Vides itaque," he writes in 1711, "charissime in Christi Fili noster, quid sancta hæc sedes,\* quid extincto Cardinali debeas, cujus sanguinis vox clamat ad te de terrâ." Had he followed up the words of his previous letters by acts of vigour such as he displayed even to the excess of imprudence in the Jansenist controversy, the Legate would have soon regained his liberty: for the arrangement between the Portuguese and Chinese Governments constituted him even in his captivity a subject of Portugal and not of the Emperor. The touching panegyric which he pronounced on the death of

\* Sanctae huic sedi ?

the Cardinal might then have been changed for a joyful thanksgiving for his release. He had already affronted the Jesuits in Portugal by interdicting them from electing any new member into their body until the Quinquenni were paid.* The Pope, therefore, was in no slight degree responsible for the misfortunes which fell in such terrible accumulation on the head of his devoted Legate. We have next to consider the part which the Portuguese authorities at Macao and Goa had in these painful events. Of their extreme culpability the reader who has even superficially read the narrative of the Cardinal's imprisonment cannot entertain the shadow of a doubt. The persecutors of the Cardinal were a disgrace not only to Christianity but to humanity itself. They were acting under the belief that they were acquiring for themselves the highest place in the royal favour, and defending a prerogative which, if it ever existed, does not appear to have been acted upon before. The Chinese officials in their contrasted humanity and kind services to the Legate put to an eternal shame these betrayers of the cause, and persecutors of the servants of Christ.

We cannot but here recall the course which their countrymen pursued towards the great Xavier, which made his early death as real a martyrdom as that of Tournon, and the causes

* "Mem. Stor.," tom. viii. p. 49.

which we assigned to their hostility in the opening of our narrative. The same policy of selfish and sordid exclusiveness was carried on in all their dealings with their then extensive settlements, and Teyxeira was only carrying on the traditions of Alvarez, while the Cardinal was renewing the testimony of Xavier. The Portuguese were the natural enemies of all missionary work, foreseeing the dangers which would accrue to their trade with China if any collision with the Imperial authorities should be the result of it. The Jesuits had, with their proverbial diplomatic skill, averted, at least for a time, a danger which they must have foreseen as inevitable, if the more uncompromising Dominicans and Franciscans were to enter upon the scene. Both parties, however, were standing on the most treacherous ground, and at any moment the privileges they enjoyed might fall into other hands, or the Emperor, under the influence of other counsellors, withdraw his exclusive concessions.

We now approach the third class of those between whom the responsibility for what we may well term the martyrdom of the Legate must be distributed—the members of the Society of Jesus. Although Pereyra had remained in Portugal, and Grimaldi does not appear at Macao, their places were too well filled by the dreaded Ozorio, who deserved well the brand of infamy which marks his name in the relation of Angelita, while Pinto was as worthy a successor of Grimaldi. To these may be added Bastos, who, with Pinto, attended and subscribed the confirmation of the acts of Teyxeira, and also several other Jesuits who took a subordinate part as directors of the persecution in which the civil authorities had now become the prominent actors. But amid the ranks of the Society governed so fatally by its Portuguese members, there was one noble exception—one who remained true to the unfortunate Legate to the very last:

> "Among the faithless, faithful only he
> Faithful found."

This was the Vice-Provincial of the Order, Giuseppe Monteyro, who, in the words of Tournon, "among all his brethren whom I know has no equal, and who was the first to swear obedience to my decree."* The French Jesuits do not appear on the scene, though the intriguing Father Gerbillon, more Portuguese than French, must be classed with the most active of the enemies of the Legate. He appears to have remained at Pekin with the Jesuits who were still tolerated there, among whom was Pereyra, who is described by the author of the "Second Relation"† as having died suddenly, "*privo di tutti i sagramenti, senza*

* "Mem. Stor.," tom. i. p. 91.  † *Ibid.*, tom. i. p. 226.

*sapersi di che male,*" on Christmas Eve 1709. Ozorio followed after him in August 1710. Pinto and Bastos had, according to the statement of the Legate, succeeded to their cruel work of persecution at Macao, though he alleges that the "direction of the machine" was still in the skilled hands of Ozorio. We must read these words with some degree of caution, inasmuch as the successors of Pereyra and Grimaldi were under the absolute rule of the governor, Diego Teyxeira, who compelled them to sign his edict against the Legate. This, the friends and biographers of the Legate freely admit when they assign all the afflictions of the Legate during his captivity to the civil authorities under the Captain-General Teyxeira, and his despotic subordinate Souza de Gayo. Whether these were the tools of the Jesuits, or acted independently of them, it is not easy to determine. But we must bear in mind that the ecclesiastical question, with all its motives and methods, had fallen into the background at Macao, while political questions and commercial interests had come to the front. The Legate was now no longer charged with ritual innovations, but with the *lèse-majesté*—it was no longer his Chinese edict, but the *Patrimonio Regio*, that brought him into collision with the civil authorities. Hence it would be hardly equitable to increase the heavy burden of obloquy which rests upon the Jesuits in their earlier conflict with the Legate, by adding to it the afflictions he endured in his captivity, although in the seclusion of his prison he would naturally attribute every one of these to their first cause, and trace them to the intrigues of his first and most implacable enemies at Pekin. He expresses this conviction throughout all his letters. In his fifth, addressed to Cardinal Paolucci, he writes of the Jesuits : "Ora col braccio Cinese, ora col Portoghese mi molestano e maltrattano."* To them also he attributes the defection of the Bishops of Ascalon and Macao.

The anonymous Franciscan whose letter is given in the sixth volume of the "Memorie," tells us that he was privileged, night after night, to hear the saddening tale of the wrongs of the Cardinal and his unmerited sufferings from his own lips—sitting up until twelve o'clock at night to listen to every sad detail. But he has given us a narrative which is so virulent in its abuse of the Jesuits, whom he always describes as the "impegnati," and denounces as a body of conspirators ever plotting against the life of the unfortunate Legate, that we cannot attach to his statements the value which belongs to the narratives of Angelita and Sala, who, from a much earlier period, were associated with the Cardinal, and were his most confidential friends. It is at least unlikely that he would

* "Mem. Stor.," tom. i. p. 93.

have concealed from them the evidence of which the anonymous Franciscan claims to have been the depository. But that evidence not only receives no corroboration from those who were to the last the companions of the Cardinal, but is too dramatic and sensational in its form to enable us to receive it as trustworthy. If, during the last year and a half of his captivity, so great a freedom had been allowed to the Cardinal in regard to the visitation of his friends, the conditions of it would not have been as severe as they are represented to us by the more authentic narratives. We have in the latter no assertion of the united action of the Jesuits at Macao, no description of them as conspirators who had actually planned to murder the unfortunate victim of this long persecution, who was absolutely incapable of offering them any resistance, being friendless and powerless, in such a state of disease and infirmity as to need no other agency to bring about his death. Yet we are told of the horrible resolution which his rivals (*i suoi emoli*) had arrived at to murder him. They were, however, at that critical moment too exclusively devoted to their trade in wine and tobacco, to their lucrative business as moneylenders, and to the preservation of their real, as well as personal, property in China, to think of revenge or murder, which could bring them no pecuniary gain. The grand ideal of Father

Ricci and his followers had so entirely vanished from their minds that it may be said of them as of the Israelites, " They were mingled among the heathen and learned their works," verifying the saying of Bishop Palafox, whose persecutions by the Jesuits bore a great resemblance to those of De Tournon: " The fish has caught the fisherman, instead of the fisherman the fish " (" Il pesce ha preso il pescatore, invece che il pescatore prenda il pesce ").*

They endeavoured, but without much success, to trace all the misfortunes of the mission to the errors of the Legate himself. That these contributed in no slight degree to bring about the final catastrophe, we have already shown. But the bitter antagonism of the Jesuits, and their paramount influence over the minds of the Emperor and the Primogenito, from the first were the true causes which made it inevitable. It is true that Father Antonio Thomas attributes to the errors of the Legate and his friends at Pekin the altered relations between the Emperor and the missionaries, and insists especially upon the zeal and energy which were exhibited by the Jesuits in order to conciliate the Emperor, and to mitigate the severity of his edict against the Christians. In the case of Appiani he writes :

* " Mem. Stor.," tom. ii. p. 34.

"God is witness both of the surprise and trouble in which we were placed by the unexpected arrest of Signor Appiani, and the order of the Emperor that he should be conducted to the province of Suchuen. But in regard to the obligation which was imposed on all the missionaries, both present and future, to appear in the presence of the Emperor, and to receive from him the patents of residence, we call God again to witness how speedily we exerted all our powers for many days, in order to avert this blow, before the Emperor had published his decree. We foresaw the evil which would accrue from it to the mission, and we represented it at the palace. Prayers, supplications, entreaties, advice—all that we could do we did on the occasion. We begged an audience for one of our body—for a deputation with the object of obtaining a promise from his Majesty that he would graciously determine not to publish a decree from which we feared the most terrible consequences. The Emperor refused to see us, and made answer through the Primogenito that for the future, when we desired to propose anything to his Majesty, we should begin by addressing the Primogenito."\*

This is a specimen of the long defence of one of the most active of the Jesuit missionaries, and one who appears to have been present in most of the

---

\* "Mem. Stor.," tom. iv. p. 25; "Lo stato presente," p. 137.

scenes he describes. His letter is chiefly devoted to the causes of the Emperor's dislike, both of the Bishop and the Legate, and the errors of judgment and proofs of ignorance which so greatly offended the Court. It does not, however, deal with those personal questions between the two parties which made the schism between them so inveterate, but rather constitutes an exculpation of the Society generally, than a defence of its separate members. On this latter point there is a profound and somewhat ominous silence, though they were even accused by the Franciscan Fra Michele Fernandez of letting their houses for the basest purposes, in order to obtain more money for them (*dare ad affitto le case loro a meretrici pubbliche per ricavarne maggior profitto*). Whatever may be the feelings of suspicion and even aversion which the history of the Society has impressed upon the public mind, and which are greatly increased by the secrecy which is its first principle, and the extraordinary discipline which gives it such strength in action, we cannot but hesitate to receive *ex parte* statements so seriously inculpating it as those of the anonymous Franciscan. Of the degeneracy of the members of the order who formed the Chinese mission we have too convincing and painful evidence to suffer us to doubt it for a moment. Yet even here its extraordinary solidarity as an order, or rather army, ought not to betray us into the belief that every member of the body was equally guilty of the persecution of the Cardinal and responsible for the shipwreck of one of the greatest missionary plans which was ever devised—the death-dream of the great Xavier, the life-work of his successor Ricci, and the last death-thought of Tournon on his bed of suffering. Though we cannot venture to hope that we have done much in these pages towards the solution of this difficult historical problem, we have at least endeavoured to state the case of both the parties as fairly and fully as the conflict of witnesses in a matter which enlisted their strongest feelings and most heated passions renders it possible to do.

Before our work was quite completed the judgment of an unbiassed member of the Roman Church came accidentally under our eye, which anticipated our chief conclusions. It occurs in a memoir addressed to the Vatican Council, bearing the singular title of *Quæstio*, which was taken to Rome by Bishop Ketteler, and is believed to have been drawn up by that able and influential Prelate.

"Clement XI." (observes the writer) "and Benedict XIV., in condemning certain Chinese rites as superstitious, brought about the result which the religious orders (*religiosi*) had predicted, the destruction of that entire Church; while if, on the other hand, the method of the religious (*i.e.*, Jesuits), against whom the action was taken, had been accepted by the rest, a certain moderation would have been applied, and without any condemnation the end might have been gained, the shadow of superstition might have been purged away, and by a toleration of some degree of ritual error (*materialis erroris*) the many storms of controversy might have dissipated, peace retained, and religion preserved."\*

The writer of these words refers, in support of his conclusions, to a letter of Luquet, Bishop of Esebon, to the Bishop of Langres (Ep. ii.). The whole argument of the treatise is directed against the danger of conferring an immeasurable and irresponsible power on a single member of the Church, however exalted may be his position and claims. The fatal results which followed the exercise of this power by Clement XI., both in Europe and Asia, were a solemn warning to the Vatican Assembly, and one which was brought before them in this treatise in the most forcible manner. The retrospect which the author gives of the dangers which had ever followed from the admission of the extreme claims of the Papacy, might well have made the members of the Council to pause ere they invoked them anew, had not the intimidation which was held over the more learned

\* "Documenta ad illust. Concil. Vatican. P. I.," p. 120.

minority, and the actual terrorism exercised by the Pope himself, compelled the unfortunate dissidents to surrender, after a feeble resistance, the higher doctrines they brought with them to the Council.

Before we close our narrative, it may interest the reader to learn some of the incidents which succeeded the expulsion of the religious orders from the Empire. The illustrious Emperor, who fills so large a space in our pages, after a successful reign of sixty years, left as his heir his fourth son, his eldest and second sons, for some conspiracy, having been thrown into prison, where they died. Both these princes were personally known to Appiani, to whom we are indebted for these facts. A member of one of the religious orders, for having been involved in the same conspiracy, was strangled and burned; while the nobles who had taken part with the Jesuits against the Legate were reduced to beggary, and died in prison. The new Emperor, having liberated the innocent Father Pedrini, was induced, at the instance of Pope Benedict XIII., to set at liberty also the faithful Appiani, though, through the neglect of the governor of the province in which he was confined, he was not released till 1726, when too enfeebled by age and suffering to be able to return to his native country. His last words to his nephews, in the letter we have already quoted, were worthy of his invincible faith and constancy: "In every place and in every clime there is a way to Paradise, and to this alone we ought to aspire." *

* "Mem. Stor.," tom. i. p. 356.

www.ingramcontent.com/pod-product-compliance
Lightning Source LLC
Chambersburg PA
CBHW031449160426
43195CB00010BB/920